One Greater Man

ONE GREATER MAN

Justice and Damnation
in
Paradise Lost

Desmond M. Hamlet

Lewisburg
Bucknell University Press
London: *Associated University Presses*

© 1976 by Associated University Presses, Inc.

This work grew out of a doctoral dissertation, "Justice and Damnation in *Paradise Lost*," © 1973 by Desmond M. Hamlet.

Associated University Presses, Inc.
Cranbury, New Jersey 08512

Associated University Presses
108 New Bond Street
London W1Y OQX, England

Library of Congress Cataloging in Publication Data
Hamlet, Desmond M.
    One greater man.
    Based on the author's thesis, University of
Illinois at Urbana-Champaign, 1973.
    Bibliography: p.
    Includes index.
    1. Milton, John, 1608–1674.   Paradise lost.
    2. Milton, John, 1608–1674—Knowledge—Religion
and ethics.   3. Justice in literature.   I. Title.
PR3562.H32   821'.4   74-27670
ISBN 0-8387-1674-1

PRINTED IN THE UNITED STATES OF AMERICA

for
Barbara, Sharon, and Lawrence

Contents

Preface

I owe a great deal of thanks to a number of people. To Professor Arthur E. Barker for encouraging my interest in Milton, in the first place, and for his incomparable tutorial guidance "through all the instances of example"; to Professors U. Milo Kaufmann, Howard C. Cole, and Lawrence Jacobs for their inestimable help when help was needed most; to the Librarian and staff of Knox College at the University of Toronto for their kind assistance; to the able custodians of the invaluable Miltonic treasures in the Rare Book Room at the University of Illinois at Urbana-Champaign for their willing guidance and direction; to my good friend and confidante, Mrs. Kern W. Dickman, for her interest, advice, and practical help over the years; to my children, Sharon Elizabeth and Lawrence Lambert, for their incredible patience and restraint in dealing with a continuously harried father; and finally, to my wife, Barbara Fenella, my most severe but perceptive and instructive critic, whose willing aid and comfort sustained and strengthened me through the many years of this most delightful but demanding project—my deepest appreciation and continued gratitude!

Desmond Hamlet

Buffalo, New York

Acknowledgments

I would like to thank the following for permission to reprint copyrighted material:

The Bobbs-Merrill Company, Inc., for excerpts from *John Milton: Complete Poems and Major Prose*, edited, with notes and introductions, by Merritt Y. Hughes (copyright © 1957 by The Odyssey Press, Inc.), reprinted by permission of The Bobbs-Merrill Company, Inc.

E. J. Brill Publishing Company, for excerpts from *Calvin's Catholic Christology*, by E. David Willis. Used by permission of E. J. Brill Publishing Company, Leiden, Netherlands.

Columbia University Press, for excerpts from *Liberty and Reformation in the Puritan Revolution*, by William Haller. Used by permission of Columbia University Press.

J M Dent & Sons Ltd, for world rights exclusive of the U.S.A., to reprint material from *Puritanism and Liberty*, selected and edited, with an Introduction, by A. S. P. Woodhouse. Foreword by A. D. Lindsay. First published in Great Britain 1938. Used by permission of J M Dent & Sons Ltd, Aldine House, 26 Albemarle Street, London.

11

One Greater Man

1
Milton, the Critics, and the Justice of God

i

Although Milton is often thought to have succeeded in *Paradise Lost* in asserting Eternal Providence, he is just as often regarded as having failed to "justify the ways of God to men" (I. 26). The main reason for this view centers in the argument, most recently articulated by Lawrence Hyman, that "the universe which God has created and which He governs cannot be reconciled with human standards of reason and justice."[1] Thus, Milton's assertion of God's eternal governance of His universe is often seen as compounding the poet's basic problem of trying to make the ways of God acceptable to men. For, as William Empson argues, "if God is to be shown acting in a story, we have something better to do than take his status for granted. . . . God is on trial [in *Paradise Lost*] . . . and the

---

1. Lawrence W. Hyman, *The Quarrel Within* (Port Washington, N.Y.: Kennikat Press, Inc., 1972), p. 56.

15

reason is that all the characters are on trial in any civilized narrative."[2]

Further exacerbating the problem is the difficulty not only of Satan's very existence in the poem and his seemingly heroic opposition to the God of *Paradise Lost*, but also of the creation and existence of Hell and God's rather severe treatment of Satan—even to the point of his damnation, including his involuntary metamorphosis into a serpent in Book X. In plain terms, either Milton's God is not so omnipotent as the poet wishes us to believe, and thus is incapable of exercising total control over the world He made, or if He is omnipotent, then He is surely not so just, good, and loving as Milton claims that He is. For no God of justice, goodness, and love would indulge Himself in such harsh and unfair treatment of any of His creatures or permit the existence of such wickedness and woe, clearly antithetical to His wholesome creation and to His loving purposes.

The crux of this exasperating problem would seem to lie, most logically, in the nature of God's justice. For although Milton *tells* us that his God is just because of His essential goodness and love, God's actions in the poem do not appear to support the poet's claim. Moreover, as D. P. Walker correctly argues in another context,

> it is no way out of these dangers to assert, as Luther and the Calvinists did, that, although God's justice or goodness are not the same as ours, and consist merely in the arbitrary exercise of His will, God is nevertheless just and good. These epithets, used in such a way, lose all meaning, and are merely a device for avoiding blasphemy.[3]

The same observation aptly applies to the God of *Paradise Lost*.

---

2. William Empson, *Milton's God* (London: Chatto & Windus, 1961), p. 94.
3. *The Decline of Hell* (Chicago: The University of Chicago Press, 1964), p. 54.

It is, however, the thesis of this study that in *Paradise Lost* Milton's God needs no such excuses. For not only is He omnipotent, just, good, and loving, but His justice—which is the key to His integrity—is a vital aspect of His omnipotence, goodness, and love. In *Paradise Lost*, God's justice is an indispensable instrument of the divine creative purpose, which is continuously seeking, through the wide variety of challenges and opportunities mimetically represented in the poem, to induce in the creature an essentially creative response to the divine ways. But more than this, my argument is that in *Paradise Lost* God's justice is understood and portrayed by Milton more in terms of the essentially biblical concept of *righteousness* (from the Hebrew *zedakah*, and the Greek *dikaiosune*), with its significantly restorative and re-creative qualities, than in terms of the fundamentally Hellenistic sense of justice (brought into the developing Christian tradition by Augustine and others), with its overemphasis on the distributive and retributive nature of God's dealings with men.

Milton's vast reservoir of knowledge bears the unmistakable signs of a wide variety of influences, including Neoplatonic, Talmudic, and Kabbalistic characteristics (all of which reinforce the features of distributive and retributive justice latent in *zedakah* and *dikaiosune*). However, in *Paradise Lost*, divine justice is the cornerstone not only of the moral integrity of Milton's God, but particularly of His love and concern for all His creatures. To put it quite plainly, in Milton's poem God is just because He is good and loving and desires only the creative (or restorative) growth, based on their equally creative response and responsibility, of all His creatures.

Thus, Satan's damnation in *Paradise Lost* is the direct result both of his obduracy and of his moral degeneration—both of which, in turn, are the inescapable consequences of his self-imposed perversion of the creative and restorative process fundamentally woven into the fabric of the poem's world.

Satan is damned in *Paradise Lost* because he willfully abuses
the liberating qualities of God's justice, thus imposing upon
himself an accursed and destructive Hell. Consequently, not
only is it impossible for him after his fall to find ease for his
tortured self or any pleasure except the pleasure of destroying
(IX. 129–34; 475–79), but he has to admit, as he does on
Mount Niphates:

> Nay curs'd be thou; since against his thy will
> Chose freely what it now so justly rues.
> Me miserable! which way shall I fly
> Infinite wrath, and infinite despair?
> Which way I fly is Hell; *myself am Hell*.
>
> (IV. 71–75)[4]

Satan's damnation is infinite and inevitable because his
perversion—by which he has cut himself off from the emancipating qualities of the divine creative justice—is complete
and obdurate.

Satan's perversion is total because he obdurately repudiates
the Son of God who, by His own creative use of His freedom
and His responsibility, merges totally with the basic creative
processes of the world of *Paradise Lost*. It is in this sense that
the person and function of the Son, in whom "all his Father
shone / Substantially express'd" (III. 139–40), may best be
understood in *Paradise Lost*. For, in the final analysis, it is the
Son who functions in the poem as the Father's indispensable
instrument of His creative and restorative purposes—whether
such a function relates to the creation of the universe (as narrated by Raphael to Adam in Book VII), or to the creative
offer of His life for Man's restorative growth (in Book III), or
to His re-creative judgment of Man as "Both Ransom and
Redeemer voluntary" (X. 61).

---

4. Italics mine. All quotations from *Paradise Lost* are from *John Milton: Complete
Poems and Major Prose*, ed. Merritt Y. Hughes (New York: The Odyssey Press, 1957).

Thus, Satan is damned in *Paradise Lost* because, by re-pudiating the creative qualities of the divine justice (which is God's indispensable instrument of His creative purposes), he, in effect, repudiates the very person and function of the Son of God. This is exactly what Milton portrays Satan as doing, for example, in V. 661–71 (despite his full awareness of the Father's words in V. 611–15). By this decisive *act* of rebellion, Satan sets in motion the whole process of his self-imposed damnation, since, for man or angel alike, such contempt of the significant person and function of the Son in God's universe is the damnable and unpardonable sin.

ii

Milton's understanding of the nature and function of divine justice in *Paradise Lost* was the result of more than twenty years of vigorous efforts to clarify for himself and for his country-men the practical significance of God's relationship to men—specifically, to the English people of his own day. In the final analysis, it is Milton's conviction about the essential integrity of God's justice that underlies the entire body of his poetry and prose, and that enables him to confront, with a response firmly rooted in the incomparable justice of the di-vine ways, his own practical problems and the perplexing ecclesiastical and political difficulties of the English nation of his day. For example, it is Milton's faith in the justice of God that provides the obvious reverberations of *Areopagitica*—regarding God's constructive agency in bringing adversity and trial into the lives even of the regenerate—that we hear, in firmer and clearer tones, in *De Doctrina Christiana* and in *Paradise Lost*.

In *De Doctrina Christiana*, for example, Milton defines a good temptation as "that whereby God tempts even the righteous for the purpose of proving them"[5] and plainly reiterates his point in *Paradise Lost* in the important dialogue between Michael and Adam in XI. 358–73. Underlying both of these passages is Milton's stated premise in *Areopagitica* that in their postlapsarian condition, men bring not innocence but impurity into the world. Hence their vital need for testing and trial as an important instrument for their total nurture and growth.[6]

It is especially in connection with man's total nurture and growth that Milton understands the fundamental integrity of God's justice to stand or fall. As he correctly observes, hardly anyone will murmur against God's absolute disposal of the natural and civil actions of men, for that is clearly His right. But the "outcry against divine justice" is especially due to the erroneous supposition that God Himself disturbs the course of equity by capriciously inclining men's wills to moral good or evil, and then rewarding the good and punishing the wicked.[7] Milton insists that God's governance of the universe should rather be understood as relating to matters that are natural and civil, to "things indifferent and fortuitous," instead of to concerns of morality and religion.[8]

This is especially so because of the indispensable condition of responsibility that must characterize the lives even of the elect and regenerate, if they are to persevere successfully to the promised bliss of perfect glorification.[9] Milton spends more than two-thirds of his discussion of "Assurance and Final Perseverance" in *De Doctrina Christiana* clarifying, with typical Arminian emphasis, the conditional nature of men's salvation, and insisting that men may persevere and be assured

---

5. Book I, Chapter VIII (*The Student's Milton*, ed. Frank Allen Patterson [New York: Appleton-Century-Crofts, Inc., 1961], p. 984).
6. See Hughes, *John Milton: Complete Poems and Major Prose*, p. 728.
7. Patterson, p. 1000.
8. *Ibid.*
9. See Patterson, p. 1021.

of God's supporting grace along the way, "so long as nothing is wanting on their own parts, and they continue to the utmost in the maintenance of faith and love."[10] Moreover, as Milton explains in his discussion of God's punishment of sin, if we were not, to some degree, responsible for our personal religion, the whole idea of God's entering into a covenant with us would be rather farcical.[11] Therefore, as Milton sees it, "not the elect, but those who continue to the end, are said to obtain salvation,"[12] and that salvation is not the gift of an immediate perfection, but "the ultimate object of our existence."[13] "Hence," Milton immediately adds, "the struggle between the flesh and the Spirit in the regenerate."[14] For the rest of his life, Milton never abandoned his conviction of the creature's responsibility to persevere to the end, in creative response to the instrumental divine justice.

Milton was clearly disappointed over the collapse of the Commonwealth and the consequent restoration of Charles II to the English throne.[15] By 1666, for instance, when he wrote his letter to Peter Heimbach (the only extant letter of Milton's written after the Restoration), his enthusiastic patriotism, which he had boldly displayed in his polemical writings of the early 1640s, had obviously waned, if not completely disappeared. As he informs Heimbach,

> [because of] what you call "policy," but I would rather have you call "loyality to one's country"—this particular lass,

---

10. *Ibid.*
11. *Ibid.*, chapter 12.
12. *Ibid.* chapter 25.
13. *Ibid.* chapter 21.
14. *Ibid.*
15. John Diekhoff suggests that "by October [of 1659], in the *Letter to a Friend concerning the Ruptures of the Commonwealth*, his hopes are definitely waning . . . and in March 1660, in the *Ready and Easy Way to Establish a Free Commonwealth*, he has come to regard the days before the inevitable Restoration as a 'shroving-time' before a 'long Lent of servitude'" (see John S. Diekhoff, *Milton on Himself* [London: Cohen & West, Ltd., 1965], p. 179).

after inveigling me with her fair name, has almost expatriated me, so to speak.[16]

To conclude, however, that Milton's disillusionment (even compounded by the constant hardships and dangers to which he was then exposed)[17] bitterly turned into a distrust in divine Providence or to an utter self-pity that led to a drastic revision of the important religious principles he always held dear is to misunderstand the real post-Restoration Milton whose intense religious awareness produced *Paradise Lost*.

Once again, Milton's letter to Peter Heimbach offers a clue. In this very letter in which Milton evidently sheds his zealous pre-Restoration patriotism, he attributes his safety to divine Providence:

> by the blessing of God, who had provided for my safety in a country retreat, I am still both alive and well, nor useless yet, I hope, for any duty that remains to be performed by me in this life.

That this is no glib religious commonplace becomes obvious just a few lines later when Milton informs Heimbach that he (Milton)

> should dread a too numerous progeny from so many forms of the marriage-union as you enumerate, were it not an established truth that virtues are nourished most and flourish most in straitened and hard circumstances.[18]

Twenty-two years after *Areopagitica*, and "straitened and hard

---

16. "Familiar Letter 31," in Diekhoff, p. 274.

17. Jonathan Richardson tells us that apart from suffering severe private losses financially, Milton "was in Perpetual Terror of being Assassinated, though he had Escap'd the Talons of the Law, he knew he had Made Himself Enemies in Abundance. He was So Dejected he would lie Awake whole Nights" (*The Life of Milton, and a Discourse on Paradise Lost*, 1734, in *The Early Lives of Milton*, ed. Helen Darbishire [London: Constable & Co., Ltd., 1932], pp. 275–76).

18. Diekhoff, p. 274.

circumstances" notwithstanding, Milton is still seriously committed to that fundamental principle:

> that which purifies us is trial, and trial is by what is contrary.[19]

Throughout his life, Milton resolutely refused to compromise on one fundamental point: *the integrity of the justice of God.* Even when, following the collapse of the Commonwealth and the restoration of Charles II, he was faced with disillusionment and adversity, Milton continued to insist on God's unimpeachable justice. As he informs us in *Defensio Secunda,* "I had not been without my share of human misery," immediately adding, "but . . . I had, at the same time, experienced singular marks of the divine regard."[20] Already we can recognize the basic traits of that indomitable faith which was later to express itself in the memorable words which mark the close of his poetic career:

> All is best, though we oft doubt,
> What th' unsearchable dispose
> Of highest wisdom brings about,
> And ever best found in the close.
> (*Samson Agonistes*, ll. 1745–48)

What occurs during the interim is, despite its complexity, the unfaltering effort of a faithful poet-prophet to

> assert Eternal Providence,
> And justify the ways of God to men.
> (*PL*, I. 25–26)

"Yet even believers," Milton once wrote, "are not always

19. Patterson, p. 738.
20. *Ibid.*, p. 1139.

sufficiently observant of these various operations of divine providence, until they are led to investigate the subject more deeply."[21] Believers or not, this is precisely what we should, in fairness to Milton, or at least, in the interest of objective criticism, now proceed to do.

iii

Among the many engaging critical works on *Paradise Lost* during the last two decades or so, Lawrence Hyman's recent study of art and morality in Milton's poetry, *The Quarrel Within*,[22] focuses, to some extent, on what Hyman calls "the inexplicability of God's justice."[23] In terms reminiscent of G. Rostrevor Hamilton's well-known study of Milton's Satan,[24] Hyman suggests that the main conflict in *Paradise Lost* arises from the fact that God's ways, including His justice, cannot be reconciled with human standards of reason and logic. However, unlike A. J. A. Waldock, William Empson, J. B. Broadbent, John Peter, R. J. Z. Werblowsky, and other critics of *Paradise Lost* whose studies agree at least in principle with Hyman's premise,[25] Hyman argues that "this contradiction between God's ways and our human values is not a weakness in the poem but the source of its dramatic power."[26] Despite his ostensibly positive view of Milton's art, however, Hyman

---

21. *Ibid.*, p. 984.

22. Hyman argues the interesting thesis that in order to appreciate Milton's major poems, we need not divorce the art from the morality—"take the poetry and let the religion go, as many readers believe"—but we should see the moral philosophy not as dogma but "as an integral part of the imaginative experience" (Hyman, p. vi).

23. *Ibid.*, p. 71.

24. *Hero or Fool?* (Folcroft, Pa.: The Folcroft Press, Inc., 1944); reprinted 1969.

25. See Waldock, *Paradise Lost and Its Critics* (Cambridge, England, 1947); Empson, *Milton's God* (London, 1961); Broadbent, *Some Graver Subject: An Essay on 'Paradise Lost'* (New York: Schocken Books, Inc., 1967); Peter, *A Critique of Paradise Lost* (Hamden, Conn., 1970); and Werblowsky, *Lucifer and Prometheus: A Study of Milton's Satan* (London, 1952).

26. Hyman, p. 56. In his essay on Satan, Hamilton, observing "a notable division between Milton the sensuous and passionate, and Milton the moralist," insists that the

finds it more than a little difficult to accept either Milton's idea of God or the concept and function of divine justice in the poem. Instead, he casts his critical vote for the obduracy and recalcitrance of human experience in the face of "the inexplicability of God's justice."

Endorsing the application of a viable contextualist aesthetics to *Paradise Lost*, Hyman forcefully argues in favor of a proper appreciation of the imaginative experience of the poem in terms of the dramatic tension created by both Milton's doubts and his certainties. This is the source of the poem's strength, Hyman argues, and "if we accept this duality in the rhythmic pattern as central to the action, we can respond to the poem without reference to our moral presuppositions," since those presuppositions will have been absorbed "in the poetic experience, in the tragic irony of the action, just as Milton's religious feelings were absorbed by the intractable myth."[27]

Clearly, Hyman's own theory of poetry is perceptive and essentially liberating, and he is correct to insist that

> both the writing and the reading of great literature does involve *a capacity for going beyond our personal feelings in order to enter into another kind of experience.*[28]

But surely such an aesthetic experience must, to be valid, be true for us all, and would seem, most logically, to preclude preconceptions about "the stubborn intractability of experience"[29] and the "inexplicability of God's justice," as well as the distinctly religious feelings of both the writer and the reader. For, even if we assume the possibility of such objectivity for writer or reader, it should be clear that such a premise

---

cleavage does not amount to a split personality, "for short of complete harmony, the two sides can and do work together, and then only do we have in a full sense Milton the poet" (Hamilton, pp. 37–38).

27. *Ibid.*, p. 73.
28. *Ibid.*; italics mine.
29. *Ibid.*

requires a capacity for going beyond personal feelings of every sort (including even a predisposition to avoid making moral responses of any sort) in order to enter into the *total* aesthetic experience through our involvement with a work of art. Despite his commitment to contextualist criticism, Hyman fails, I suggest, to do just that.

Admittedly, the greatness of a poem does not necessarily lie in its power to inculcate a moral feeling. Yet, it is equally true that the level of experience that emerges from a great work of art may be indispensably informed by what Rajan calls "a certain awareness of tradition, a certain 'given' structure of values and responses [that] are taken for granted by the movement of the poem,"[30] and that—it is not unreasonable to suggest—should at least be respected in terms of the significance of those very contextual postulates. Further, when such a work of art happens to be *Paradise Lost*, it is more than likely that a narrowly pedantic, impressionistic approach "may be more provincial than the narrow historicism it tries to overcome."[31] J. E. Seaman is right that it is entirely possible that the modern reader will enlarge his experience more "by the difficult process of adjusting his view to Milton's than by having Milton retailored."[32]

Milton's poetry, because of its fusion of content and form (of *dogma* and *drama*), is, in fact, constantly working away from the accidental and the contingent in human affairs, from an obdurate individuation (a recalcitrance of experience, if you will), toward an extraordinary apprehension of reality, a transcendent level of experience. Stanley Fish's insight, in his recent comment on Russell Fraser's assessment of Milton's poetry, is especially instructive in connection with the "inex-

---

30. *Milton's Paradise Lost: Books I and II*, ed. Balachandra Rajan (New York: Asia Publishing House, 1964), p. xxii.
31. John E. Seaman, *The Moral Paradox of Paradise Lost* (The Hague: Mouton & Co. N.V., Publishers, 1971), p. 10.
32. *Ibid.*

plicability of God's justice."[33] For in this context, the so-called inexplicability of God's justice must begin to define itself, through the upward-tending Poetry, in terms that are increasingly comprehensible, even if transcendent. For it, too, moves upward toward an unveiling of what, from an existentialist perspective, is perhaps a mystery, but of what progressively is thrown into sharper relief as the finite questing mind pursues the goal of union with infinite reality at the highest level of transcendental experience. The successful result is that the seemingly incomprehensible divine justice is now clearly understood for what, in fact, it always was: an instrument of the divine creative purpose.

Thus, if the moral beliefs in Milton's poetry, both explicit and implicit, are seen as being subjected to an experience within the poem that contradicts them in some essential way, it is only because we persist in driving a wedge, however surreptitiously, between Miltonic dogma and drama. Moreover, to begin with such a premise is almost inevitably to end with the irreconcilable dichotomy between "the need to find justice in His ways and the full portrayal of His arbitrary nature"[34] instead of with the organic union of the medium and the message, which logically resolves itself into a partial appreciation, at least, of the poem's complexity in portraying its God and His justice.

E. M. W. Tillyard and Arthur Barker are only two of the many critics of *Paradise Lost* who have recognized the crucial importance of Milton's fusion of dogma and drama in his major poem. Tillyard, for example, clearly appreciates Milton's fusion of his theology and his poetry in *Paradise Lost*, as is evident from his suggestion that

---

33. Stanley E. Fish, "Inaction and Silence: The Reader in *Paradise Regained*," *Calm of Mind: Tercentenary Essays on Paradise Regained and Samson Agonistes in honor of John S. Diekhoff*, ed. Joseph Anthony Wittreich, Jr. (Cleveland, Ohio: Case Western Reserve University Press, 1971), pp. 26–27.
34. Hyman, p. 115.

Milton's theology, far from being a tie, an alien thing, was a great world of thought where an immensely wide range of passions could find their natural embodiments.[35]

Consequently, not only is Tillyard convinced that "there is no major flaw in the poem," but also that it is "now more than ever out of the question" that Milton either consciously or unconsciously conceived of Satan as the hero of *Paradise Lost*. Suggesting that the chief point of the *crisis* of the poem is "the delusion of Satan and the ironic defeat of his apparently gigantic efforts by the small decencies of the human pair," Tillyard insists that to regard Satan as the hero of *Paradise Lost* is tantamount to arguing that "the author of the Book of Samuel was really on the side of Goliath against David."[36]

Unfortunately, Tillyard's grasp of Milton's fusion of dogma and drama collapses when it is related to the difficult issue of divine justice in *Paradise Lost*. Although he readily admits the difficulty of one's being sure about "Calvin or Perkins or some other Puritan divine rather than St. Paul or St. Augustine in speaking of whence Milton derived his version of central Christian dogma,"[37] Tillyard willingly suggests that Milton's extreme emphasis on the legalistic side of redemption, as well as his emphasis on Christian Liberty, appears to ally him with the Calvinists. Tillyard sees the tremendous hold of this severe Calvinistic legalism on Milton in the two most pertinent but difficult passages in *Paradise Lost* where Milton discusses the issue of God's justice: the celestial colloquy in III. 80–343 and Michael's conversation with Adam in XII. 285–465, both of which deal with the same theological matters—and in the

---

35. *Milton* (London: Longmans, Green & Co. Ltd., 1952), p. 31. Cf. L. A. Cormican's similar observation in "Milton's Religious Verse," *The Pelican Guide to English Literature: From Donne to Marvell*, ed. Boris Ford (Baltimore, Md.: Penguin Books, 1956), p. 176.
36. *Studies in Milton* (London: Chatto & Windus, 1960), pp. 51–52.
37. *Ibid.*, p. 160.

same unemotional and unenthusiastic tone. It is especially this last fact that encourages Tillyard's suspicion of "the possibility of strain" in the two passages.[38] Tillyard concedes that in XII. 285–306, "the legalistic side of the doctrine is successfully fused with the ardour with which Milton describes the state of filial liberty,"[39] but he remains convinced that

> Milton was powerless either to free himself from, or to impassion, the legalism that then for all Christians, but especially for the Puritans, was inseparable from the doctrine of the Redemption.[40]

Although a discussion of the celestial colloquy in Book III, which Tillyard cites, has to be postponed to a more convenient section of this study, we can focus at this point on the passage in Book XII that Tillyard sees as portraying (as he does the passage in Book III) the legalism of the redemptive process. Despite his general understanding of the poet's fusion of dogma and drama in *Paradise Lost*, Tillyard fails to appreciate Milton's essentially biblical concept of redemption in terms of the liberating function of the Son. By fulfilling (or more accurately, "filling full") God's justice—through what Tillyard correctly calls "filial liberty"—the Son changes the apparent legalism of the process of redemption into a genuine emancipation from what would otherwise remain a severe and impossible juridical process.

This is precisely the point of Michael's explanation to Adam in XII. 285–306, which sums up the relationship of the Gospel to the Law, and which Tillyard correctly cites, along with his approval of Rajan's commentary on these significant lines.[41] Tillyard is quite right that this passage is "Milton's

---

38. *Ibid.*, p. 161.
39. *Ibid.*, p. 166.
40. *Ibid.*, p. 164.
41. *Ibid.*, pp. 165–66.

definitive exposition of the doctrine (of filial freedom) as applied to fallen man."[42] He is correct also that the legalistic side of the doctrine is successfully fused with "the ardour with which Milton describes the state of filial liberty." However, he fails to appreciate the extent to which "the legalistic side of the doctrine is successfully fused" with the ardour of Milton's description of filial liberty.

Michael's meaning is clear. Because "sin / Will reign among them" (ll. 285–86), the Law was given to them "to evince / Thir natural pravity, by stirring up / Sin against Law to fight" (ll. 287–89). However, because the Law "can discover sin, but not remove" (l. 290), the sinful will come to see that "Some blood more precious must be paid for Man" (l. 293),

> Just for unjust, that in such righteousness
> To them by Faith imputed, they may find
> Justification towards God, and peace
> Of Conscience.
>
> (XII. 294–97)

These lines, along with the concluding lines of the passage (ll. 303–6), constitute the heart of the passage, and Tillyard is quite right to observe that this great doctrine of filial liberty "was one which Milton not only absorbed from his Puritan upbringing but felt in his blood."[43] It is hard to understand, however, how one can celebrate either the theological content or the poetic expression of these two sections of the passage (ll. 294–97 and ll. 303–6) without recognizing the crucial significance of the intervening lines (ll. 298–302), which not only provides the vital theological connection between ll. 294–97 and ll. 303–6, but contributes, with an equal poetic significance, to the developing rhythmic and emotional crescendo of the entire second half of the passage.

---

42. *Ibid.*, p. 165.
43. *Ibid.*, p. 166.

Theologically, the *legalistic, subjective* nature of the Law is clear:

> which the Law by Ceremonies
> Cannot appease, nor Man the moral part
> Perform, and not performing cannot live.
> So Law appears imperfet. . . .
>
> (XII. 297–300)

But so is its *re-creative, instrumental* function:

> *and but* giv'n
> With purpose to resign them in full time
> Up to a better Cov'nant, disciplin'd . . . .
>
> (XII. 300–302)

Paradoxically, the Law has both a *legalistic, subjective* nature and a *re-creative, instrumental* function—a fact that Milton meticulously takes into account with his use of the succeeding conjunctions in line 300, not merely for the sake of the iambic pentameter, but also for the purpose of emphasizing the significant theological point at stake here. Milton's meaning is, I suggest: So the Law appears imperfect, and *yet* was given for the purpose of leading sinful men at the right time, disciplined, to a Covenant much better than the preceding imperfect arrangement.[44]

Poetically, these intervening lines regarding the nature and function of the Law are beautiful and forceful. Not only do they function as an important bridge between ll. 294–97 and ll. 303–6, thus occupying a significant place in the entire "emotional" second half of the passage, but few readers can miss the impressive position, as well as the compelling force, of "disciplin'd" at the end of line 302, with its double function

---

44. Cf. Gal. 3:24: "Wherefore the law was our schoolmaster to bring us unto Christ, that we might be justified by faith."

of reaching both back to ll. 300–302 and forward to the rest of
the passage.

The point is that ll. 297–302 are as much a part of Milton's
enthusiastic description of the state of filial liberty as ll.
294–97 and ll. 303–6. What Tillyard fails to appreciate (despite his observation that "the legalistic side of the doctrine is
successfully fused" with Milton's enthusiastic description of
the state of filial liberty) is the extent to which that very state
of filial liberty *depends* on the process of redemption, and not
vice versa. Moreover, he fails to appreciate the extent to which
"the legalistic side of the doctrine" becomes transformed,
through the Son's restorative submission to that very "legalistic side of the doctrine," into an equally noninjurious and
indirectly emancipating process. This is exactly the point that
Michael later makes in his continuing discussion of the
Savior's redemption of mankind:

> But by fulfilling that which thou didst want,
> Obedience to the Law of God, imposed
> On penalty of death, and suffering death,
> The penalty to thy transgression due,
> And due to theirs which out of thine will grow:
> So only can high Justice rest appaid.
>
> . . . .
>
> But to the Cross he nails thy Enemies,
> The Law that is against thee, and the sins
> Of all mankind, with him there crucifi'd,
> Never to hurt them more who rightly trust
> In this his satisfaction.
>
> (XII. 396–419)

Tillyard's failure to understand the restorative, instrumental nature and function of God's justice in *Paradise Lost* causes
him not only to misunderstand the emancipating qualities of
the divine justice as it operates in and through the Son (who,

incidentally, is quite prominent in both of the indicated passages in Book III and Book XII) but, further, to misrepresent Milton's complex use of his poetic fusion of dogma and drama in *Paradise Lost*. This Arthur Barker does not do.

Like Tillyard, Barker believes that Milton's "essential dogmas . . . demand dramatic constitutions for their adequate expression."[45] However, Barker does not stop there. Recognizing the "organic relation between the poem's message and its medium,"[46] Barker pursues this mutual dependence of dogma and drama in *Paradise Lost* to the crux of Milton's complex poetics, which he finds in the poet's theological concept of regeneration and in his very theory of poetry. But more than that, Barker insists that Milton's "theory of renovation and his theory of poetry are, at the responsive and responsible heart of the matter, quite inseparable."[47] Thus, he sees the world of *Paradise Lost* as essentially dramatic, characterized by the continuous interaction of the divine creative purpose and the creature's response, which, in turn, is actualized by inevitable, dynamic relationships—and so, by conflict. It is this constant conflict, Barker believes, that makes the world of *Paradise Lost* so dramatic.

However, because of their fundamental, "organic relation" in *Paradise Lost*, both dogma and drama, Barker insists, are intended to serve the common goal of a creative response in terms of the creature's active participation in, and his restorative imitation of, the divine ways. In fact, for Barker, the divine ways themselves often operate, even ironically, in *Paradise Lost* to induce in all of God's creatures the proper, creative response to those very divine ways, including God's

---

45. *"Paradise Lost:* The Relevance of Regeneration," in *Paradise Lost: A Tercentenary Tribute*, ed. Balachandra Rajan (Toronto: University of Toronto Press, 1969), p. 77.
46. *Ibid.*, p. 67.
47. "Structural and Doctrinal Pattern in Milton's Later Poems," *Essays in English Literature from the Renaissance to the Victorian Age*, ed. Millar MacLure and F. W. Watt (Toronto: University of Toronto Press, 1964), p. 194.

justice and even the existence of woe in men's postlapsarian situation. As he puts it, in connection with the Dialogue in Heaven in Book III,

> our difficulties with Milton's God would be greatly lessened if we recognized and adequately appraised the dramatic role which the Father purposely adopts in order to challenge the Son and to induce from him a loving and sacrificial response, as his ways challenge all beings to make creative use of proferred opportunity.[48]

Consequently, Barker has no difficulty with the supposed harshness of Milton's God in Book III, for instance, since he understands the Father's entire role during the Council in Heaven as a purposely adopted stance in order to induce from the Son a loving and creative response.[49]

Barker's position is sound and demonstrates a significant understanding of Milton's complex poetic style. In this context also, divine justice (as do all the divine ways) operates in an essentially instrumental manner to effect the creative (or re-creative) response of the creature to God's unchanging creative purpose for him. Thus, divine justice becomes a part of the divine love which, in turn, motivates the total divine creative purpose for the creature, in effect making the often rigid demands of God's ways more comprehensible, if not necessarily acceptable.

While acknowledging Barker's important insight, I am suggesting that in *Paradise Lost* Milton develops a representation of divine justice that goes much further than the mere comprehensibility of the divine ways in their dealings with the creature. My argument is that in Milton's poem God's justice

---

48. "The Relevance of Regeneration," p. 68.
49. See especially "The Relevance of Regeneration," pp. 67–70, for an engaging discussion of God's ways as purposely instrumental in inducing in all His creatures the proper, creative response.

is the same as His *righteousness* and possesses more of an essentially restorative and liberating quality than the erroneously overemphasized characteristic of distribution and retribution.

Although Barker correctly understands God's justice in *Paradise Lost* as an indispensable instrument in the re-creative processes of the poem's world, he does not explicitly define justice in terms of its primarily restorative and re-creative quality because he does not fully explore the direct relationship between the nature and function of God's justice in the poem and the person and function of the Son. I am arguing that in *Paradise Lost* God's justice is indeed an indispensable instrument of the divine creative purpose, but that it is also much more than that.

In *Paradise Lost*, divine justice lies at the very heart of the creative and restorative processes of the poem's world because of its inherent and inextricable connection with the Son, in whose person and function, throughout the poem, God's righteousness or justice is most fully expressed. In fact, not only is the Son (in His person and function as the indispensable instrument of God's creative and restorative purposes) *like* God's justice (in its nature and function as the indispensable instrument of God's creative and restorative purposes), but more significantly, the Son *is* God's justice. Thus, to understand the person and function of the Son is to understand the nature and function of God's justice, and to appreciate the nature and function of God's justice we must first appreciate the person and function of the Son. For, in the final analysis, it is the Son, in *Paradise Lost*, who is the best exemplification and actualization of the justice of God.

iv

With such a reading of the nature and function of divine justice in *Paradise Lost*, a number of problems in the poem become much less perplexing and incomprehensible. For example, the Dialogue in Heaven in Book III (which Tillyard correctly regards as one of the most difficult sections of the poem, and which will be dealt with fully in a later chapter of this study)[50] becomes much less difficult to understand. For, from the perspective of this thesis, the generally assumed dichotomy between the Father's motives and the Son's intentions disappears in the fusion of their mutual concern for Man's re-creative recovery. Moreover, as the actualization of God's righteousness in the poem, the Son becomes both the means and the end of God's justice for Man's restoration.

By His creative response to the Father's equally creative purpose for both the Son's growth and Man's restoration, the Son dramatically endorses, as Milton makes clear, every aspect of the Father's intention and role in this scene. For example, not only does the Son, in His very first words in this scene, recognize the Father's ultimately creative intention for Man (III. 144–45), but the Father carefully reassures the Son (as Milton no doubt wishes to remind us) that there is not—and has, in fact, never been—the slightest disharmony between the Father's motives and the Son's intentions for Man. As the Father puts it at the beginning of His second speech,

> O Son, in whom my Soul hath chief delight,
> Son of my bosom, Son who art alone
> My word, my wisdom, and effectual might,
> All hast thou spok'n as my thoughts are, all
> As my Eternal purpose hath decreed.
>
> (III. 168–72)

Indeed, as the only one who is willing and able to give His life for Man's restoration to life, the Son dramatically confirms both the indispensability and the efficacy of the paradoxically demanding and emancipating divine justice. In short, by His

---

50. Tillyard, *Studies in Milton*, pp. 160 and 162.

sole sacrifice for Man, the Son confirms His own person and function as the best expression of that very justice which is demanding that very sacrifice for Man's restoration.

From this perspective, even the Father's seemingly harsh decree in III. 210 (which Empson labels "the stage-villain's hiss" in which "God is much at his worst here, in his first appearance")[51] confirms the person and function of the Son as God's justice. Empson offers the plausible stylistic suggestion that the Father "needs to be [at his worst here], to make the offer of the Son produce a dramatic change."[52] The problem with Empson's reading is that, according to the text of Milton's poem, the Son's dramatic offer does not alter, but confirm, the Father's intention. This, in fact, is the poet's intention throughout the Dialogue in Heaven, and indeed, throughout *Paradise Lost,* as the similar colloquy between the Father and the Son at the beginning of Book XI suggests.

For example, in His speech during which He presents the prayers of the penitent Adam and Eve and intercedes with the Father on their behalf, the Son pleads with the Father (XI. 40–42) *not* to reverse His decree in X. 48–54, which ends with the remarkable words:

Justice shall not return as bounty scorn'd.

As the Son puts it in XI. 40–42,

> till Death, his doom (which I
> To mitigate thus plead, not to reverse)
> To better life shall yield him. . . .

In terms of Empson's reading of III. 210, the Son's request should be the exact opposite of what, in fact, He asks. But the Son, whose request, Milton tells us just a few lines later, was

---

51. Empson, p. 120.
52. *Ibid.*

what the Father decreed (XI. 47), is saying exactly what the
Father decreed not only in X. 54, but in III. 210 as well. And
He says this for a very valid reason: He both effects and is the
Justice of God—which first condemns Man for his sin, and
then liberates him through the willing death of the Son Him-
self.

In the end, the so-called stage-villain's hiss (which Empson,
for his own purposes, isolates from its context) turns out to be
an important part of the indispensable and efficacious condition for Man's restoration by the Son. For what the Father
actually says during His second speech in Book III is:

> Die hee or Justice must; *unless for him*
> *Some other able, and as willing, pay*
> *The rigid satisfaction, death for death.*
>
> (III. 210–12)

In terms of the thesis that I am proposing here, some of the
preceding lines in the Father's second speech in Book III,
which Empson regards as apparently invented for the specific
purpose of "setting a reader's teeth on edge" (11. 198–201),
also become more comprehensible. As the expression of God's
justice, the Son exists and operates at the very center of the
creative and restorative processes of the poem's world, and
thus is the unavoidable point of reference for all relationships
in *Paradise Lost*. This is why, I suggest, Milton portrays the
Father as exalting the Son in Book V (11. 600–615) and as
appointing Him "Vicegerent," to whom, as He declares in
Book X,

> I have transferr'd
> All Judgment, whether in Heav'n, or Earth, or Hell.
>
> (X. 56–57)

Consequently, the Son serves as the moral point of reference
not only for all relationships among the creatures of *Paradise*

Lost, but also for the inescapable relationships between those creatures and Himself. That is to say, it is impossible for any creature in the poem's world to avoid relating to the Son, either positively or negatively. To those who relate to Him positively, He brings salvation; but to those who relate to Him negatively, He brings damnation, since to negate the significance of the Son Who exists at the center of the poem's world is to repudiate the central creative and restorative focus of the world of *Paradise Lost.*

It is in this context that the meaning of III. 198–201 and the whole question of God's "hardening the heart" or "blinding the understanding" should be understood. In an important discussion of this difficult concept in *De Doctrina Christiana,* Milton argues that

> as God's instigating the sinner does not render him the author of sin, so neither does his hardening the heart or blinding the understanding involve that consequence; inasmuch as he does not produce these effects by infusing an evil disposition, but on the contrary by employing such just and kind methods, *as ought rather to soften the hearts of sinners than harden them.* First, by his long-suffering. . . . Secondly, by urging his own good and reasonable commands in oppoition to the obstinacy of the wicked.[53]

The similarity between this passage and III. 198–201 is clear.

However, the point becomes clearer when the whole question of God's "hardening the heart" or "blinding the understanding" is examined in its proper context, as it should be, of the existence of evil and the fact of damnation in *Paradise Lost.* For if God is responsible for the one, He is obviously responsible for the other. Moreover, it is easy to conclude that He is, in fact, responsible for the existence of evil and woe and for the creature's obduracy and repudiation of the divine prefer-

---

53. Book I, chapter 8.

ences if we deal with the question as an isolated, metaphysical issue unrelated to the poem's postulates and poetic representations, including the Son of God as the actualization and expression of God's justice. On the other hand, if—as I am arguing—we recognize that an important feature of the universe of *Paradise Lost* is God's justice, and that that justice achieves its fullest and most effective expression in the person and function of the Son, then it is not difficult to recognize that evil, obduracy, degeneration, and damnation are all the inevitable, self-imposed consequences of the creature's repudiation of the creative and restorative ethos of the universe of *Paradise Lost*. To put it quite simply: in *Paradise Lost*, the creature who is not saved does not wish to be saved. But more than this, the creature who does not wish to be saved automatically imposes upon himself the only possible alternative in the poem's world—that he be damned.

Having said that, however, we must still face the perplexing question of the *origin* of evil in *Paradise Lost*, especially when we confront the fact of the existence of Hell, which features so prominently in the poem, or when we encounter such a seemingly inscrutable passage as the lines in Book II where the poet tells us:

> A Universe of death, which God by curse
> Created evil, for evil only good,
> Where all life dies, death lives, and Nature breeds,
> Perverse, all monstrous, all prodigious things,
> Abominable, inutterable, and worse
> Than Fables yet have feign'd, or fear conceiv'd,
> *Gorgons* and *Hydras*, and *Chimeras* dire.
>
> (II. 622–28)

On the surface, the lines appear to suggest that God created an evil "universe of death," further implying the possibility (in keeping with what Milton tells us in the poem about God's omnipotence) of His being the origin of evil. However, several observations are in order here.

However much he wishes to preserve the omnipotence and sovereignty of his God in *Paradise Lost*, Milton, we can be sure, would hardly suggest that God is responsible for the entrance of evil into the universe of *Paradise Lost*. Indeed, he tells us quite plainly elsewhere in the poem that Satan is the "author of evil" (VI. 262). Moreover, Milton's inclusion of "*Gorgons and Hydras, and Chimeras* dire" in the "universe of death" would seem to suggest his allegorical interpretation of these monsters "as representing the pangs of guilty consciences," as Merritt Hughes reminds us that he did in *Prolusion I*.[54] The idea of guilt as the basis for this "universe of death" is reinforced in the passage by the characteristic perversity that dominates the evil "universe of death," further reinforced by the subtle interplay on death, life, and the perversion of the good in a similar treatment in IV. 194–204.

More important than all of this, however, is Milton's comment in *De Doctrina Christiana* on Isaiah 45:7: "I make peace and create evil":

> that is, what afterwards became evil, and now remains so; *for whatever God created was originally good, as he himself testifies, Gen.i.*[55]

"Nor does God make that will evil which was before good," Milton further explains,

> but the will being already in a state of perversion, he influences it in such a manner, that out of its own wickedness it either operates good for others, or punishment for itself.[56]

---

54. *John Milton: Complete Poems and Major Prose*, ed. Merritt Y. Hughes (New York: The Odyssey Press, 1957), p. 247n.
55. Book I, chapter 8; italics mine.
56. *Ibid.*

Milton's most important statement, for the purposes of this discussion, is his observation that "whatever God created was originally good." This is exactly the impression we get from Raphael's description of the Creation to Adam in Book VII, as Adam attests by his demeanor and comment in VIII. 1–13. The goodness of God's creation also underscores the severity of the effect on Nature of Eve's moral transgression— described by the poet in IX. 780–85, where the words *rash, evil, wound, sighing, woe, lost, slunk,* and *guilty* in such a short passage of merely six lines leave us with the feeling of profound tragedy over all of God's creation. This is as it should be, since at the matrix of the universe of *Paradise Lost* is the "high / Creator" (VIII. 12–13), the Source of the creative energy that pervades the poem's entire world and that actualizes itself (through the person and function of the Son) in the characteristic creative and restorative processes of *Paradise Lost*.

Thus, any breach of that characteristic in the poem's world brings into existence the physical and moral antithesis of the creative and restorative processes that activate the universe of *Paradise Lost*. In *Paradise Lost*, Hell is the accursed and destructive antithesis of Heaven and the result of Satan's accursed and destructive breach of the creative order. In such a context, it is highly unlikely that Milton would ascribe to his poem's God (the Source of all creative and restorative good in *Paradise Lost*) the very origin of evil. Nor is it reasonable—in the context of the poem's pervasive and determinative creative and restorative processes—that we can hold the God of *Paradise Lost* responsible for the creation of evil because He is omnipotent. Finally, we should not allow ourselves to forget that, in Milton's poem, Hell is ultimately the psychological process of a moral degeneration into the irreversible state of an accursed damnation. As Milton puts it, in his description of Satan in this regard,

                              for within him Hell
He brings, and round about him, nor from Hell
One step no more than from himself can fly
By change of place.
                                        (IV. 20–23)

Or as Satan even more convincingly concludes,

Which way I fly is Hell; myself am Hell;
And in the lowest deep a lower deep
Still threat'ning to devour me opens wide,
To which the Hell I suffer seems a Heav'n.
                                        (IV. 75–78)

William Empson mischievously suggests that Milton might
well have answered the critics of his poem's God "that it was
not his immediate business to invent a new theology."[57] There
is more truth to Empson's remark than meets the eye, and I
am quite prepared to accept his suggestion in regard to this
analysis of Milton's concept of God's justice in *Paradise
Lost*—with one important qualification: Milton's concept is
not based on "what goes on in the minds of Christians"[58]—of
any brand! Rather, it is based on what he understood to be
going on, regarding this subject, in both the Old and the New
Testaments.

---

57. Empson, p. 94.
58. *Ibid.*, p. 93.

2

Justice and Damnation in Seventeenth-Century Puritanism

i

With the biblical aberrations of the early Judaizing Christians (see, e.g., Gal. 2:11–16) and with the doctrinal contributions of such Fathers of the Church as Chrysostom, Lactantius, Ambrose, and Augustine to the emphasis on legalism in general and on the vindictive nature of God's justice in particular, the fallacy of divine punishment as the sole objective of God's justice became firmly established in the developing Christian tradition. By the time of the theological excesses of John Calvin in the sixteenth century and the rise of Puritanism in England in the seventeenth century, the concept of the distributive and retributive nature of God's justice was considerably reinforced by the moralistic and theocratic tendencies of even such a generally respected preacher and theologian as the Puritan moderate Richard Baxter, as well as, for example, the doctrinally orthodox William Prynne and William Ames on the one hand, and the Antinomians John Eaton and John

44

Saltmarsh on the other. It is to Milton's credit that although he was deeply embroiled in constant religious controversy between 1641 and 1660, he was able ultimately to avoid these moralistic, theocratic, and antinomian excesses and to develop his concept of God's justice on the basis of the fundamental beliefs of the Old and the New Testaments.

It is of more than passing interest that the thinkers and writers of his day who come the closest to Milton's own concept of divine justice are the Independent John Goodwin, and the essentially Nonconformist Cambridge Platonists, all of whom—including Milton—are basically Arminian and rationalist in their understanding of God's relationship to men. Even so, Milton is truly the Independents' Independent and exemplifies in the seventeenth century a virtually singular fusion of biblical accuracy and humanistic concerns. James Holly Hanford is right when he argues that

> Milton's true kinship is not with Bunyan or Baxter, nor yet altogether with Cromwell and the heroes of the battle for religious and political liberty, but with those men of the older day, whose spiritual aspirations were united with the human passion for truth and beauty and who trusted the imagination as an important medium for the attainment of their ideals. . . . The point is often overlooked by those who, focusing their view on his Puritanism, conceive of him as a poet for the Puritans. Orthodox theology in the eighteenth century did indeed derive some support from *Paradise Lost*, but no one surely will claim that Milton came to his own as a champion of the dying cause of Calvinism.[1]

Indeed, Milton's significance in seventeenth-century thought is the direct result of his repudiation of "the dying cause of Calvinism" in its major emphases. For example,

---

1. *John Milton: Poet and Humanist* (Cleveland, Ohio: The Press of Western Reserve University, 1966), pp. 163–64.

whereas Calvinism views human nature as almost irretrievably depraved because of man's natural corruption after the Fall, Milton's understanding of God's restorative work in man is firmly rooted in Christ's function as the re-creative means not only of healing man's natural corruption, but also of providing him with the enlightened discernment to realign himself gradually and progressively with the creative processes of the universe (cf. *Paradise Lost* III. 175–97). It is especially this synthesis regarding the progressive growth of the regenerate through their renewed powers, their enlightened senses, and their continued and disciplined response to their "Umpire *Conscience*,"

> *whom if they will hear,*
> Light after light well us'd they shall attain,
> And to the end persisting, safe arrive,
> (III. 195–97)[2]

which is so sadly missing in the theological systems of orthodox, moderate, and even sectarian Puritanism during the seventeenth century.

Chronologically, John Calvin (1509–1564) does not, of course, fall within the seventeenth century. However, in terms of the impact of his ideas on Puritan thinking, Calvin's basic views are woven into the very fabric of seventeenth-century Puritan theology. As A. S. P. Woodhouse points out, Calvinism (especially in terms of Calvin's ideal of the "holy community") is "the main seed-ground of the Puritan movement."[3] And M. M. Knappen, in his discussion of "Puri-

---

2. Italics mine.
3. *Puritanism and Liberty* (London: J. M. Dent and Sons, Ltd., 1938; reprinted 1965), p. [36]. Regarding the Puritan ideal of the "holy community," Woodhouse points out that "the active presence of this ideal of the 'holy community' (however divergent the inferences in theory and practice therefrom) appears to me to furnish the only satisfactory basis for a working definition of Puritanism. . . . The acceptance of the ideal bespeaks a common element in all Puritan thought"(*Ibid.*, p. [37]).

tan Theology," correctly observes that "Calvin cast such a deep shadow over the Puritan world that he determined the tone of its entire thinking."[4]

With this last comment Holmes Rolston would probably not completely agree. For, in his provocative discussion of the fundamental differences between Calvin and the Westminster Confession, Rolston does acknowledge that "the proponents of the theology of the Westminster Confession" see in Calvin "grist for their mill"; however, Rolston insists that "what is for Calvin a half-truth becomes for the Calvinists the substructure of their classical creed."[5] According to Rolston,

> never in all Christian thought has the contrariety between righteousness and grace been so sharply drawn as in Reformed theology of the seventeenth and eighteenth centuries. The contrast, which had preceded in scholastic usage, and from which Luther and Calvin had escaped at the cost of a Reformation, now returns with a double vengeance.[6]

With this appropriate cue, Rolston cogently disputes any real affinity between Calvin's basic theological emphasis and "the twin covenant tectonics which dominates the substructure" of both "the Westminster Confession of Faith in 1646" and "all later Reformed dogmatics."[7] To Rolston, Calvin retains in his soteriological emphasis "one of the richest insights of the Ref-

---

Woodhouse's observation is well taken; however, it ought also to be pointed out that underlying the Puritan ideal of the "holy community" is the even more fundamental notion of a desirable theocracy for the government of the affairs of men, which, in the first place, is informed by a self-righteous insistence on God's arbitrary, absolute, and unconditional predestination of the elect to be both the select society of saints and the nucleus of the larger corrigible community.

4. *Tudor Puritanism: A Chapter in the History of Idealism* (Chicago & London: The University of Chicago Press, 1939; reprinted 1965), p. 376.

5. *John Calvin versus The Westminster Confession* (Richmond, Va.: John Knox Press, 1972), p. 80.

6. *Ibid.*

7. *Ibid.*, pp. 11 and 13.

ormation," since the Reformer understands the justice or righteousness of God as a "saving righteousness."[8]

Despite Rolston's sympathetic interpretation of Calvin's theology, however, it is more than a little difficult to dismiss "the strongly predestinarian Calvin" and not to conclude, with Rolston, that "Calvin's theological determinism is not satisfactory, especially as it is clouded by a 'secret counsel' from which reprobation flows."[9] Even more regrettable is the considerable extent to which Calvin's "theological determinism" (with its " 'secret counsel' from which reprobation flows") affects his entire theological system. For one thing, we must wonder with E. David Willis whether Calvin's particular theological determinism does not "put in question the priority of revelation and therefore the weight of the revelation of God in the particular person of Jesus Christ."[10] For, despite the clearest evidence that Calvin indeed understood "communion with Christ" to be "a testimony sufficiently clear and strong" that such persons "are written in the book of life,"[11] Willis is quite right that

> why it [God's decision to restore the world and reconcile men to himself] is a twofold, eternal decision of salvation or damnation for each individual, and why the particular revelation in Christ should hasten men to their predestined end . . . is seemingly not known from the incarnate Lord. Here is where Calvin unfortunately advances too boldly, in spite of the pastoral context and reverence for the mystery which persistently characterize his treatment of the doctrine of predestination.[12]

8. *Ibid.*, p. 85.
9. *Ibid.*, p.30.
10. *Calvin's Catholic Christology* (Leiden, Netherlands: E. J. Brill Publishing Company, 1966), p. 117.
11. John Calvin, *Institutes of the Christian Religion* (III, xxiv, 5), trans. John Allen, vol.2 (Philadelphia: The Westminster Press, 1936): 224. Cf. John S. Coolidge, *The Pauline Renaissance in England* (Oxford: Oxford University Press, 1970), pp.135–36n.
12. Willis, p. 117. Cf. *ibid.*, pp. 67–73, and especially pp. 153–54, where, among other things, Willis suggests that the "extra Calvinisticum" in Calvin's theology tends

Indeed, it is Calvin's concept of an eternal divine decree, which predestines some to election and others to damnation in a particular and absolute manner, that impugns the very foundation of all significant divine-human relationships: the goodness and justice of God. Such a doctrine not only deprives men of their constitutive capacity for responsible choice, but also implies a God who is at best capricious, and at the worst irresponsible, tyrannical, and wicked.

At the heart of Calvin's doctrine of predestination is his insistence on God's "supreme rule of justice," informed and sustained by "the pure will of God alone."[13] It is in God's pure will, Calvin suggests, that we must seek "the ground of the distinction" between the reprobate and the elect. For God's pure will is "the supreme and primary cause of all things," including the fact "that Adam should fall from the unimpaired condition of his nature"; that "while we are elected in Christ, nevertheless that God reckons us among his own is prior *in order* to his making us members of Christ"; that "while the elect receive the grace of adoption by faith, their election does not depend on faith but is prior *in time and order*"; that "all the deeds of men are governed"; and even that "the reprobate remain in their blindness *or be deprived of such portion of faith as is in them.*"[14] Yet, argues Calvin,[15] "God cannot be called the cause of sin, nor the author of evil, nor subject of any guilt." "They are ignorant and malicious," Calvin insists, "who say

---

"to reinforce Calvin's occasional minimization of the importance of Christ's bodily presence during his earthly ministry; the invisible behind the visible flesh receives disproportionate attention. Were this route systematically pursued, something Calvin fortunately does not do, the saving character of God's manifestation *in the flesh* would be seriously qualified. This in turn would go ill with Calvin's simultaneous affirmation of the goodness of our tangible world and our concrete humanity as created" (p. 153).

13. John Calvin, "Articles concerning Predestination,"*Calvin: Theological Treatises*, trans. J. K. S. Reid, The Library of Christian Classics, vol. 22 (Philadelphia: The Westminster Press, 1954): 179.

14. *Ibid.*

15. Regarding the authorship of "Articles concerning Predestination," see Reid, pp. 19 and 178.

that God is the author of sin, since all things are done by his will or ordination; for they do not distinguish between the manifest wickedness of men and the secret judgments of God."[16]

The thrust of the "Articles concerning Predestination" informs Calvin's discussion of predestination in his *Institutes of the Christian Religion*. For example, in his analysis of what he entitles "Election Confirmed by the Divine Call. The Destined Destruction of the Reprobate Procured by Themselves,"[17] Calvin argues that

> as the Lord, by his effectual calling of the elect, completes the salvation to which he predestinated them in his eternal counsel, so he has his judgments against the reprobate, by which he executes his counsel respecting them. Those, therefore, whom he has created to a life of shame and a death of destruction, that they might be instruments of his wrath, and examples of his severity, he causes to reach their appointed end, sometimes depriving them of the opportunity of hearing the word, sometimes, by the preaching of it, increasing their blindness and stupidity.[18]

Calvin's point (with its harsh, uncompromising tone) is much the same here as it is in the "Articles concerning Predestination."

Calvin's unflinching sense of God's inscrutable, though justifiable, sovereignty leads not only to the Reformer's insistence on the twofold nature of God's eternal and absolute decree, but also to Calvin's categorical refusal to discuss the dynamics of responsibility—human or divine. For instance, in connection with the coming of the Messiah "to the posterity

---

16. *Ibid.*, pp. 179–80.
17. *Institutes*, 3: xxiv (Allen, pp. 217–41).
18. Allen, p. 232.

rather than to their ancestors," Calvin insists that

> he will torment himself in vain, who seeks for any cause of
> this beyond the secret and inscrutable counsel of God. Nor
> need we be afraid lest any disciple of Porphyry should be
> imboldened *to calumniate the justice of God by our silence in its
> defense.* For while we assert that all deserve to perish, and it
> is of God's free goodness that any are saved, enough is said
> for illustration of his glory, so that every subterfuge of ours
> is altogether unnecessary.[19]

Even where he is willing to make a partial concession to some
sense of responsibility on man's part, Calvin quickly pulls
away from any significant engagement of the issue, resting his
case entirely on what he calls the "just but inscrutable judgment of God":

> That the reprobate obey not the word of God, when made
> known to them, is justly imputed to the wickedness and
> depravity of their hearts, provided it be at the same time
> stated, that they are abandoned to this depravity *because they
> have been raised up,* by a just but inscrutable judgment of
> God, *to display his glory in their condemnation.*[20]

Calvin is biblically correct when he contends, in his final
statement of this section of his *Institutes,* that "it is acting a
most perverse part, to set up the measure of human justice as
the standard by which to measure the justice of God."[21] However, in his insistence on the "just but inscrutable judgment of
God" as "the supreme and primary cause of all things," Calvin
appears entirely to have overlooked the devastating effect such
divine arbitrariness imposes on the creature—both in terms of
a total annihilation of human freedom and in terms of an

---

19. *Ibid.*; italics mine.
20. *Ibid.*, p. 235; italics mine.
21. *Ibid.*, p. 241.

inevitable denigration of the physical and the natural. Stefan Zweig senses the full impact of such a theology on the human situation:

> Wishing to elevate the divine as high as possible above the world, Calvin threw the worldly down into the lowest depths. Wishing to give supreme dignity to the idea of God, he degraded the idea of man. . . .
> Obviously one who, from the philosophic standpoint, regards man as an unsuccessful and abortive piece of workmanship on God's part will never be willing, as theologian and statesman, to concede that God can have given such a creature a jot of liberty and independence.[22]

Calvin's "Brief Reply in refutation of the calumnies of a certain worthless person," directed at Sebastian Castellio (1515–1563), confirms the thrust of Zweig's observation.

During a brief visit with Calvin at Strasbourg in 1540, Castellio was invited to conduct the college at Geneva. However, he was evidently refused ordination after his arrival in Geneva because of his opinion of the biblical Song of Songs as a *carmen lascivium et obscaenum*, among other supposed theological heresies. Requested to leave, Castellio went to Basel, where he lived out the remainder of his days and from where his attacks on Calvin and the Church at Geneva were conducted.[23] J. K. S. Reid correctly observes that "the nature of Castellio's attack on Calvin's *Predestination* appears clearly enough from the reply it elicited."[24] For instance, in the very first paragraph of Calvin's "Brief Reply" (evidently written in 1557),[25] one gets a fairly clear sense of Castellio's position regarding the justice of

---

22. *The Right to Heresy: Castellio against Calvin*, trans. Eden and Cedar Paul (New York: The Viking Press, 1936), p. 53.
23. See Reid, p.331.
24. *Ibid.*, p. 332.
25. Reid suggests, for instance, that when three small works attacking Calvin's doctrine of predestination came in succession to Calvin's notice, Calvin, suspecting

God, which he refuses to associate with a "secret counsel" responsible for evil and sin:

> There has come to my notice the foolish writing of a worthless individual, who nevertheless presents himself as a defender and vindicator of the glory of God, because *he contests the principle that God rules the world so that nothing happens but by his secret counsel.* This wretched fellow does not see that, by snatching at false pretexts *for excusing the justice of God,* he thereby subverts his power. This is just as if he were to try to rend God himself in pieces. For the rest, to give colour to his sacrilege, with as much malice as wickedness *he remarks in his preface that God is not the cause of evil, nor wills sin.* As if, when we attribute supreme dominion to God, we call him the author of sin![26]

Although Calvin tries generally, in his "Brief Reply," to maintain the third person in referring to himself, he is so far from being dispassionate that he clearly identifies the authorship of the piece:

> It is worth while to see what he says by way of refutation. He charges *me* with attributing inconstancy to God.[27]

Castellio's charge of inconstancy on the part of Calvin's God is based, in part, on Calvin's insistence on God's *double will.* As Calvin puts it in his "Brief Reply,"

> concerning the double will of God, which Calvin, after Augustine and other pious teachers, attributes to God, this good critic says that he marvels at such childish talk. . . . Afterwards he adds that this distinction was

---

Castellio's authorship, "replied at once and sharply to the first two, criticizing both matter and writer; and to the third at greater length in the following year, 1558" (p. 332).

26. *Ibid.*, p. 333; italics mine.
27. *Ibid.*, p.338; italics mine.

thought out by us, because otherwise we should have lain open to the charge of blaspheming God.[28]

Much more significant is Castellio's observation, reported by Calvin, that Calvin and his followers "say that Adam sinned by the will of God, and that the impious not merely by God's permission but by his impulse perpetrate all their wickedness. . . . [But] how can it be that God willed this, when he had created Adam *in his own image?*"[29] To such an incisive and crucial comment—involving the whole cluster of theological concerns regarding man's rational consciousness, his sense of moral responsibility, and his capacity for transcendent, spiritual experience—Calvin lamely answers:

As if it were for me to render a precise reason for the hidden judgments of God, so that mortal men might understand to a nicety that heavenly wisdom, whose height they are commanded to adore.[30]

Calvin tacitly admits precisely the meaning of Castellio's accusation, as is made much clearer toward the conclusion of his "Brief Reply":

Moreover, to extricate himself the better, he puts forward free will as shield, denying that it is astonishing that God does not hinder men acting by free impulse as seems good. *But why does he inflict upon us this term fabricated out of nothing?* Scripture everywhere declares that man is captive, servant and slave of the devil, is carried away by all his inclinations into vice, and is unable to understand what the things of God are, let alone perform them.[31]

28. *Ibid.*
29. *Ibid.*, p.336; italics mine.
30. *Ibid.*
31. *Ibid.*, pp. 342–43; italics mine.

By a subtle extension of his belief in the natural depravity of man, Calvin clearly fails to recognize any sense of human freedom in moral and spiritual affairs. But more than this, by his insistence—which we have seen—on the total control of all human endeavors by the divine will (especially in its *secret counsel*) Calvin further refuses to recognize any necessary capacity in the creature for good. In the end, goodness and freedom, for Calvin, are the exclusive prerogative and possession of his God. It is hardly surprising that in 1855 Henry Cole translated the "Brief Reply to Castellio" as "Calvin's Calvinism."[32]

ii

The reason for Henry Cole's witticism in 1855 seems totally to have escaped the orthodox Puritans of the seventeenth century. William Prynne, for example, has left us, in his *Anti-Arminianism* of 1630, a classic illustration of Puritan orthodoxy's adoption of "Calvin's Calvinism." Prynne's oppressive intolerance was, moreover, to express itself fifteen years later in his notorious *Truth Triumphing over Falshood* (with its incredible title of approximately one hundred and twenty words), to be surpassed in tone and style two years later only by the abhorrent arrogance of his shorter *Sword of Christian Magistracy Supported: Or a Full Vindication of Christian Kings and Magistrates Authority Under the Gospell, To punish Idolatry, Apostasy, Heresie, Blasphemy and obstinate Schism, with Pecuniary, Corporall, and in some Cases with Banishment, and Capitall Punishments.*[33] Haller accurately sums up Prynne's personality when he explains that Prynne "was at once a grotesque caricature and the antithesis of Selden. . . . since he

---

32. *Ibid*, p. 345.
33. William Haller, *Liberty and Reformation in the Puritan Resolution* (New York: Columbia University Press, 1955), pp. 236–37.

had lost his ears in the cause of right, he could not possibly ever be wrong. Disagreement was outrage; . . . dissenters of all persuasions must give way or be exterminated."[34]

Prynne's arrogance was the direct result of his Calvinistic orthodoxy, unequivocally spelled out in his *Anti-Arminianism* of 1630, and appropriately listed by Woodhouse, in *Puritanism and Liberty*, under "The Privileges of the Saints."[35] To Prynne, he was clearly among God's elect, "which number can neither be augmented nor diminished," since "God from all eternity hath, by his immutable purpose and decree, predestinated unto life, not all men, not any indefinite or undetermined, but only a certain select number of particular men." This is the first of "seven dogmatical conclusions" at which Prynne arrives in his definition of anti-Arminianism. As in the case of "Calvin's Calvinism," Prynne's Calvinism also revolves around the central fact, stated in his fourth "dogmatical conclusion," that *"there is not any such free will*, any such universal or sufficient grace communicated unto all men, whereby they may repent, believe, or be saved if they will themselves."[36]

This is true, Prynne believes, of both the elect and the reprobate. Such "free will" is nonexistent because it is unnecessary. Regarding the elect, "though they sometimes fall through infirmity into grievous sins, yet they never fall totally nor finally from the habits, seeds, and state of grace." As for the reprobate, they clearly do not stand the slightest chance of any possible restoration, for

> though sin be the only cause of damnation, yet the sole, the primary cause of reprobation or non-election (that is, why God doth not elect those men that perish, or why de doth pass by this man rather than another, as he rejected Esau

---

34. *Ibid.*, p. 237
35. Woodhouse, p. 232
36. *Ibid.*; italics mine.

when he elected Jacob) is the mere free will and pleasure of God, not the pre-vision, the pre-consideration of any actual sin, infidelity, or final impenitency in the persons rejected.[37]

The logical consequences of such haughty self-righteousness are explicitly reported by Daniel Neal in his *History of the Puritans:*

> Prynne was foremost in this inglorious contest [the Westminster Assembly's "opposition to the toleration of sectaries"]. Forgetful of his own sufferings, he transferred to the cause of intolerance the same zeal, intrepidity, and unwearied diligence, as had distinguished him in a better service. His publications were numerous, and all were directed to the one great end of his party, the suppression of sects and the triumph of Presbytery. 'Up, therefore,' said the fiery advocate of the Covenant, in one of his addresses to Parliament, 'and be doing justice to some few chief offenders of this kind, for the present, to prevent execution upon many others, if not ruin on us all, for the future, and God himself, no doubt, will be with you; and not fear what flesh can do unto you, or sectaries speak or write against you.' (*A Fresh Discovery of some Prodigious New Wandering, Blasting Stars,* &c., *Epistle dedicatory,* 1645)[38]

Quite appropriately, among the series of publications attacking Prynne and the Presbyterians in 1645, set off by John Goodwin's *Calumny Arraign'd and Cast* on January 31 of that year, were Richard Overton's *The Araignement of Mr. Persecution,* published anonymously on April 8, and Henry Robin-

---

37. *Ibid.*, pp. 232–33.
38. *The History of the Puritans, or Protestant Nonconformists; from the Reformation in 1517, to the Revolution in 1688; comprising an Account of their Principles; their Attempts for a farther Reformation in the Church; their Sufferings; and the Lives and Characters of their most considerable Divines.* Reprinted from the Text of Dr. Toulmin's Edition: with his Life of the Author and Account of his Writings. Revised, Corrected, and Enlarged, with additional Notes by John O. Choules. 2 vols. (New York: Harper & Brothers, 1843), vol. 2, Part III, chapter 6, p. 18n.

son's *The falsehood of Mr. William Pryn's Truth Triumphing*
on May 8.[39] In every significant respect, Prynne was one of
the most disdainful of Calvinists during the seventeenth century.

Far less fanatical than Prynne, though equally committed to
Calvinist orthodoxy in the seventeenth century, was the orthodox Puritan William Ames. As Keith Sprunger points out,
"for William Ames, Puritanism was the stuff of life. The Puritan word led forth as a lamp to his feet and a light to his
path."[40] Yet, Karl Reuter sees Ames as "the leading theologian
in the awakening of reformed pietism";[41] and Sprunger also
observes that "in zeal and spirit Ames was the child of Perkins
and the spiritual brotherhood; they were his cloud of
witnesses."[42] Certainly, Ames's major works, *Medulla Theologiae (The Marrow of Sacred Divinity)* and *De Conscientia (Conscience),*[43] move far beyond the narrow, arrogant pronouncements that characterize the writings of William Prynne.
At the same time, Sprunger is quite right that

> in the main points Ames was a Calvinist of the most or-
> thodox sort, a man of the Synod of Dort. His dogmatics was
> the Canons of Dort; he had no quarrels with any of the
> famous five points—unconditional election, the limited
> atonement, total depravity, irresistible grace, and the perse-
> verance of the saints.[44]

39. See Haller, p. 378
40. Keith L. Sprunger, *The Learned Doctor William Ames* (Urbana, Chicago, London: University of Illinois Press, 1972), p.8.
41. *William Ames; the leading theologian in the awakening of reformed pietism,* trans.
Douglas Horton (Cambridge, 1965). German ed.: Neukirchen, Neukirchener Verlag,
1940.
42. Sprunger, p. 147.
43. Sprunger explains that the *Medulla Theologiae* was "one of the most published
Protestant theological treatises of the century" (p. 127). The first complete Latin
edition of the *Medulla* was published in 1627, whereas the first English editions "were
published in 1642, when two editions appeared, with two additional editions in 1643"
(p. 128; see also p. 128n). *De Conscientia,* commonly referred to as *Cases of Conscience,*
was first published in 1630 while Ames was teaching at Franeker (see Sprunger, p. 166).
44. Sprunger, p. 128.

Ames's slightly modified, but not essentially altered, Calvinist orthodoxy may be seen, for example, both in his subscription to seventeenth-century Covenant theology and in his concept of the place of natural law in the relationship between God and men. Knappen informs us, for instance, that in the seventeenth century, Covenant theology—which he calls "that modification of the original high Calvinism"[45]— "assumed considerable importance in the teaching of Perkins' student, William Ames, and through him it was passed on to Preston and Sibbes in England, to Cocceius in Holland, and to practically all the seventeenth-century New England Puritans."[46] And Sprunger explains that "in the history of theology Ames systematized, dichotomized, and charted the covenant."[47]

As a student of the pastoral William Perkins, Ames held as one of his fundamental concerns the practical business of everyday Christian living, as his interest in "cases of conscience" attests. Like Perkins before him, and like Richard Baxter after him, Ames was preoccupied with fundamental questions of practical divinity. In his *De Conscientia*, for example, Ames suggests that conscience works in man "to the end that it may be a rule within him to direct his will,"[48] and in his discussion of questions of salvation in Book II, he not only suggests that a man may know certainly what state he is in, but also insists that a man ought, with all diligence, to inquire into his situation.[49]

Obviously, such practical possibilities imply at least a sense of moral responsibility on the part of both man and God, if not also man's essentially free will, and would appear even to

---

45. Knappen, p. 395
46. *Ibid.*
47. Sprunger, p. 151.
48. *Conscience*, I, I, 3 (cf. Sprunger, pp. 169–70).
49. *Ibid.*, II, I (cf. Sprunger, p. 171).

suggest that Ames was much more rationalist than voluntarist in his understanding of the basic relationship between God and men. In fact, Sprunger explains that Ames "did leave room in his philosophy of conscience for the counsels of right reason, prudent men, and nature."[50] Yet, Ames's understanding of men's exercise of conscience is informed by his basic definition of conscience, which he believes to be "a mans judgement of himself, *according to the judgement of God of him.*"[51] Moreover, for Ames, the practical business of everyday Christian living, though not totally devoid of right reason and prudence, *"is the submissive performance of the will of God for the glory of God."*[52] Sprunger's assessment of the matter is accurately stated:

> Ames's covenant was not a bargaining covenant. The Ames covenant was as Calvinist as Calvin and placed no restrictions whatever on God.[53]

Ames's modified voluntarism, the idea of men's *ultimate* submission to the divine will, underlies his concept of the place of natural law in the relationship between God and men. Focusing on the concept of justice, Ames suggests, in *De Conscientia*, that the idea of "right" (*jus* in Latin) is properly divided into "divine" and "human." "Divine right," in turn, "is divided into right natural and right positive," both of which were "in the mind of God from eternity." However, because positive right "is not so easily apprehended by human reason, therefore it is not usually termed the law eternal." At any rate, positive right "is mutable and various *according to God's good pleasure,*" whereas "the right natural is always the same and

---

50. Sprunger, p. 169.
51. *Conscience*, I, I; italics mine. Cf. Sprunger, p. 169.
52. *The Marrow of Sacred Divinity*, II, I, 1; italics mine. Cf. Sprunger, p. 168.
53. Sprunger, p. 150.

like itself, and for this reason also it is called the law eternal."[54] This immutable "right natural" is, in fact, "natural law," and

> is that which is apprehended to be fit to be done or avoided, out of the natural instinct of natural light; or that which is at least deduced from that natural light by evident conse- quence. So that this right partly consists of practical prin- ciples known by nature, and partly of conclusions deduced from those principles.[55]

Ames suggests, moreover, that

> it is called eternal in relation to God, as it is from eternity in him. It is called natural as it is engrafted and imprinted in the nature of man by the God of nature.[56]

Further, in discussing the question of "what proportion the Moral Law bears to the Law of Nature," Ames explains that "all the precepts of the Moral Law are out of the law of na- ture," except that which determines the Sabbath and which comes from the positive law. Among the reasons that Ames gives for this significant observation is the fact that

> there is nothing in them which is not so grounded upon right reason but it may be solidly defended and maintained by human discourse; nothing but what may be well en- joined from clear reason.[57]

Once again, Ames's view appears much more rationalist than voluntarist. For he leaves us with the impression that men may well arrive at the knowledge of God's will and live such lives as will glorify Him through the diligent exercise of right reason. Ames has, however, by no means abandoned his

---

54. See Woodhouse, p. 187; italics mine.
55. *Ibid.*
56. *Ibid.*
57. *Ibid.*, p. 190.

basically voluntarist position. Although he acknowledges that such a situation might have been possible without the Fall, he nevertheless insists that such is the impairment of human reason since the Fall that nowhere is there to be found "any true right practical reason, pure and complete in all parts, *but in the written law of God* (Psalm 119:66)."[58] As he explains,

> ever since the corruption of our nature, such is the blindness of our understanding and perverseness of our will and disorder of our affections, that there are only some relics of that law remaining in our hearts, like to some dim aged picture, and therefore by the voice and power of God it ought to be renewed as with a fresh pencil.[59]

For Ames, the instrument to effect that renewal is "the written law of God" which, in terms of its singular efficacy, is tantamount to "the divine positive right [that] is a right added to the natural by some special revelation of God,"[60] and that negates the essential freedom of men within the compass of the liberating responsibilities of the eternal "right natural." To put it another way: in such a scheme, the human faculties of reason and will are not only permanently precluded from recovering their former efficient capacity for free, responsible choice, but are also now smothered in the grip of a *new*, oppressive legalism. Thus, however modified Ames's view of the covenant and of the law of nature, the implications for both the idea of divine justice and the related concept of damnation are much the same as they are for the theological system of John Calvin or for that of William Prynne. In the end, Ames's fundamental theological perspective is informed by the crucial concept of God's arbitrary imposition of His will upon the lives of men.

---

58. *Ibid.*; italics mine. In the King James Version, Psalm 119:66 reads: "Teach me good judgment and knowledge: for I have believed thy commandments."
59. *Ibid.*
60. *Ibid.*, p. 187.

The Puritan belief in the earnest application of "the written law of God" to men's daily lives also characterizes the theology of the Puritan moderate Richard Baxter. Indeed, Baxter is an excellent example of what Woodhouse regards as the Puritan's "overwhelming sense of one's responsibility to use every effort for advancing the kingdom of God."[61] But Baxter was no fanatic, and Haller is quite right that Baxter "was in the unhappy position of one who in a time of crisis seeks to promote reform and yet avoid extremes and conserve essentials."[62] When we add to that the fact that Baxter was, in a sense, caught between the two extremes of Antinomianism, on the one hand, and the Roman Catholic theology of works-righteousness, on the other, it is not difficult to see why he is generally regarded as perhaps the most *moderate* of Puritans during the seventeenth century.

For example, Thomas Jenkyn, in his "Essay on Baxter's Life, Ministry, and Theology," has the highest praise for "the eclectic Baxter."[63] Jenkyn suggests, for instance, that

> in the breadth and the depth of theology as a science, Baxter had no divine of his age that surpassed him: perhaps the truth would warrant the assertion, that in breadth and depth, he had no equal to him.[64]

Jenkyn observes that Usher was probably equal to Baxter in the depth of theological dogmatics and probably surpassed him in general knowledge, and that Jeremy Taylor was probably equal to Baxter in the breadth of scholastic literature and perhaps surpassed him "in the brilliancy of amassed thoughts." However, "Baxter is more profound than Taylor,

---

61. Woodhouse, p. [44].
62. Haller, p. 197.
63. Richard Baxter, *Sermons*, ed. Thomas W. Jenkyn (London: Thomas Nelson, 1846), p.xlv.
64. *Ibid.*

and more comprehensive than Usher." Even among the Non-conformists "there were many who excelled him in some things; as Owen in Greek exegesis, Howe in loftiness of thought, Goodwin in evangelical savour, and Flavel, in gentle sweetness but none of them equalled him in all."[65]

Indeed, Baxter's "eclecticism" ranges all the way from caustic pronouncements of doom against the unbeliever to a virtually antinomian confidence in the anticipated bliss of the afterlife. For example, in his classic sermon on Ezekiel 33:11, "A Call to the Unconverted to Turn and Live," Baxter urges that

> nature itself doth teach us all, to lay the blame of evil works upon the doers; and therefore when we see any heinous thing done, a principle of justice doth provoke us to inquire after him that did it, that the evil of the work may return the evil of shame upon the author.[66]

Baxter's "lex talionis" concept of divine justice is especially aimed at the unconverted, against whom he invariably rises with righteous indignation:

> But do you not know, that the means do lead unto the end? and that God hath by his righteous law concluded that ye must repent or perish? . . . Would you not rebuke the folly of a thief or murderer that would say, I will steal or kill, but I will not be hanged; when he knows, that if he do the one, the judge in justice will see that the other be done.[67]

Baxter never wavers in his certainty of God's just damnation against "the contemners of his grace," even indicating at times an element of justifiable spitefulness as part of the unbeliever's doom, as he does in "Making Light of Christ and Salvation," a

---

65. *Ibid.*
66. *Ibid.*, p. 69.
67. *Ibid.*, p.126.

powerful sermon on Matthew 22:5 ("But they made light of it"):

> And this will aggravate their misery, that Christ whom they set light by must be their Judge, and for this sin will he judge them. . . . You that cannot make light of a little sickness or want, or of natural death, no, not of a tooth-ache, but groan as if you were undone; how will you then make light of the fury of the Lord, which will burn against the contemners of his grace![68]

For the believer, however, the situation is entirely different, Baxter earnestly believes, as he clearly illustrates in *The Saints Everlasting Rest*. Underlying Baxter's analysis is his fundamental theological opinion (based, in part, on Rom. 8:34,35; Matt. 28:18; John 13:3; and John 9:22, 23, and 27) that "Christ's judging power according to his human nature, is not the principal, primitive, supreme; but only the supreme delegate derived power."[69] On the basis of this belief, Baxter argues that

> if our Judge were our enemy, as he is to the world, then we might well fear. If the devil were our judge, or the ungodly were our judge, then we should be condemned as hypocrites, as heretics, as schismatics, as proud, or covetous, or what not? But our Judge is Christ, who died; yea, rather, who is risen again, and maketh request for us . . . . Oh what unexpressible joy may this afford to a believer, that our dear Lord, who loveth our souls, and whom our souls love, shall be our Judge![70]

However, Baxter's confidence is hardly the result of an Antinomian indulgence in the "unexpressible joy" of salvation, devoid of any moral effort on the part of the believer. As he

68. *Ibid.*, pp.32–33.
69. Richard Baxter, *The Practical Works of Richard Baxter*, vol. 3 (London: G. Virtue, 1838): 32n.
70. *Ibid.*, p.32.

puts it in *The Divine Life,* "if the will of God be infinitely good, we must all labour both to understand it, *and perform it.*"[71] We can know the will of God, Baxter insists, if we diligently search the Scriptures:

> Search the Scriptures then, and study and inquire; for it more concerns you to know the will of God, than to know the will of your princes or benefactors, or know of any treasures of the world. The riches of grace are given to us, by God's making known the mystery of his will, according to his good pleasure which he purposed in himself, Ephes. i. 7,9. And our desire to know the good will of God, must be that we may do it.[72]

Baxter is convinced that "as worldlings study and labour for the world, and the pleasing of their flesh; so must the christian study and labour to improve his Master's talents to his use, and to do as much good as he is able, and to please the Lord."[73]

At the same time, Baxter does not understand the Christian's "study and labour to improve his Master's talents to his use" in terms of an independent human capability for moral choice. In fact, as Haller points out, a major difficulty for the moderate Baxter "was to determine 'in what sence is our Improvement of our Talent, our well doing, our overcoming . . . alledged as a Reason of our Coronation and Glory?' What is the relation of faith to works and of both to our salvation and reward?"[74] Baxter's resolution of this fundamental problem (with which he deals not only in *The Saints Everlasting Rest* [printed about 1650], but also in *Aphorisms of Justification* [1649] and in *Rich: Baxter's Confession of Faith* [1655]) begins and ends with a clear focus upon God's sup-

---

71. I, IX, 8; italics mine (*Ibid.*, p.786).
72. *Ibid.*, pp.786–87.
73. I, IX, 6 (*Ibid.*, p. 786).
74. Haller, p. 196.

reme and sovereign will, concisely outlined, for example, in *The Divine Life*.

For Baxter, "the holy perfection of his [God's]will must make us desire to have our wills conformed to the will of God."[75] Consequently,

> any thing within us that is sinful and contrary to the good-
> ness of God, should be to our souls as griping poison to our
> bodies, which nature is excited to strive against with all its
> strength, and can have no safety or rest till it be cast out.
> *And for doing good, it must be the very study and trade of our
> lives.*[76]

This does not mean, however, that men can accomplish such an objective by themselves, for "it is a most wretched absur-dity of sensual men, to try the will, or word, or ways of God, by themselves, and by their own interests or wills." Even more significantly, Baxter insists that *"the will of God is revealed in his laws, concerning the necessity of a holy life."*[77]

It is, however, precisely in terms of this *new legalism*, which discloses, in the final analysis, a rather weakened Christology, that Baxter's basic Calvinist theology is affirmed. As Jenkyn explains,

> even with Arminian divines, the Calvinistic Owen is in far
> greater acceptance than the eclectic Baxter. The reason is
> that Owen studied the Christology of Redemption more
> than Baxter; and Baxter studied the Anthropology of salva-
> tion more than Owen. Owen exhibits with much richness
> and amplitude what Christ did for the redemption of man.
> Baxter takes all this for granted, and, taking his position at
> the cross of Christ, addresses a 'Call to the Unconverted';
> *and explains and enforces the obligations of redeemed man to believe
> the testimony of God concerning his Son.*[78]

---

75. *The Divine Life*, I, IX, 6 (*Practical Works*, p. 786).
76. *Ibid.*; italics mine.
77. I, IX, 7; italics mine (*Ibid.*, p. 786).
78. Jenkyn, pp. xlv–xlvi; italics mine.

Baxter's emphasis, as indicated, for instance, in the following paragraph from *The Divine Life*, ultimately confirms Jenkyn's observation:

> Well, christians, let flesh and blood say what it will, and let all the world say what they will, judge that best that is most agreeable to the will of God; for good and evil must be measured by this will. That event is best which he determineth of, and that action is best which he commandeth. And all is naught, and will prove so in the end, that is against this will of God, what policy or good soever may be pretended for it.[79]

In his discussion "Of the Law of Christ," Edward Fisher (c. 1627–1655)—whose authorship of *The Marrow of Modern Divinity* (1645) is sometimes disputed—expresses with clarity and cogency the substance of the antinomian position regarding the important theological issue of justification. The following passage is quoted here for its value both as a concise statement of the antinomian viewpoint and as a significant contemporary comment on the crux of Baxter's theology:

> As to the point of justification, no man is, nor can be justified by the law. It is true, the Neonomians or Baxterians, *to wind in a righteousness of our own into the case of justification,* do turn the gospel into a law, properly so called: and do tell us, that the gospel justifieth as a law; and roundly own what is the necessary consequent of that doctrine, to wit, that faith justifieth, as it is our evangelical righteousness, or our keeping the gospel law, which runs thus, He that believeth shall not perish. . . . But the Holy Scripture teacheth, that we are justified by grace, and by no law, nor deed, or work of a law, properly so called, call it the law of Christ, or the gospel law, or what law one pleaseth: and thereby faith itself, considered as a deed or

79. *The Divine Life*, I, IX, 7 (*Practical Works*, p. 786).

work of a law, is excluded from the justification of a sinner, and hath place therein, only as an instrument.[80]

Ironically, Fisher accuses the Baxterians (appropriately called here *Neo*nomians) of exactly that theological lapse of which the Baxterians, as indeed all Puritans, accused the Roman Catholics: the desire "to wind in a righteousness of our own into the case of justification." To the average antinomian, the Baxterians fell into the unfortuante error of turning the free grace of Christ into a *law* of Christ, with all the damning nomological implications of the old dispensation. As John Eaton insists in his book *The Honey-Combe of Free Justification* (1642),

> if we call unto people for Sanctification, zeale and works, the fruits of the same, only with legal terrours, not putting under the fire of justification, we shall either but little move them, or else with a constrained sanctity, make them worse hypocrites, twofold more the children of hell than they were before (Matt. 23:15).[81]

And in his imaginative dialogue "betwixt Evangelista, a minister of the gospel, Nomologista, a Prattler about the law, and Neophitus, a young Christian,"[82] Fisher has Evangelista declare:

> Ay, but neighbour Nomologista, as I told my neighbour Neophitus and others not long since, so I tell you now, that

---

80. *The Marrow of Modern Divinity; containing both first and second parts. Part first. Touching both the covenant of works and the covenant of grace. In a dialogue betwixt Evangelista, a minister of the gospel, Nomista, a legalist, Antinomista, an Antinomian and Neophitus, a young Christian. Part second. Touching the most plain, pithy, and spiritual exposition of the Ten Commandments. In a dialogue betwixt Evangelista, a minister of the gospel, Nomologista, a Prattler about the law, and, Neophitus, a young Christian.* 19th ed., with notes by Thomas Boston Montrose (London: D. Buchanan, 1803), chapter 3, p. 18.

81. (London, 1642), pp. 475–76.

82. See Fisher, *The Marrow of Modern Divinity.*

as the justice of God requires a perfect obedience, so doth it require that this perfect obedience be a personal obedience, viz. It must be the obedience of one person only. The obedience of two must not be put together to make up a perfect obedience: and indeed to say as the thing is, God will have none to have a hand in the justification and salvation of any man, but Christ only . . . . Believe it then, I beseech you, that Christ Jesus will either be a whole Saviour, or no Saviour, he will either save you alone, or not save you at all.[83]

Unfortunately, the perceptive antinomian emphasis on God's free grace to the believer through Christ too readily degenerates into an overemphasis on the divine generosity, which practically strips the believer of all sense of responsible moral and spiritual conduct, and whose chief characteristic is an unconscionable self-righteousness. For example, in Fisher's discussion of "the Law of Faith; or, Covenant of Grace," Antinomista, the antinomian character, declares:

for I do verily believe, that God, for Christ's sake, hath freely pardoned all my sins, both past, present, *and to come:* so that I am confident, that what sin or sins soever I commit, they shall never be laid to my charge, being very well assured, that I am so perfectly clothed with the robes of Christ's righteousness that God can see no sin in me at all. And therefore now I can rejoice evermore in Christ, as the apostle exhorts me, *and live merrily, though I be never so vile or sinful a creature;* and indeed I pity them that are in the same slavish condition I was in; and would have them to believe as I have done, that they may rejoice with me in Christ.[84]

Significantly, Fisher comments in a footnote at this point: "How easy is the pilgrimage from Legalism to Antinomianism!"[85] *Easy,* indeed! Notwithstanding the obviously different

---

83. *Ibid.*, chapter 3, p. 212.
84. *Ibid.*, chapter 2, p. 133; italics mine.
85. *Ibid.*, p. 133n.

route that he pursues, the antinomian ironically ends up in precisely the same theologically untenable position as the typical orthodox or moderate Puritan. For like either of them, he, too, disregards or minimizes the crucial significance, in the matter of regeneration and spiritual growth, of the human faculties of reason and will. The antinomian John Saltmarsh is a case in point.

Author of *Poemata Sacra, Latine et Anglice scripta* (1636), a slim, volume of religious poems written mostly in the "metaphysical" vein; contemporary of Benjamin Whichcote and Henry More, the Cambridge Platonists; friend of William Dell, fellow-preacher in the New Model Army; and avowed advocate of toleration and unity, John Saltmarsh firmly believed in the characteristic antinomian doctrine of the free justification of the elect. As Thomas Gataker (1574–1654) suggests about Saltmarsh, "Mr. Eaton's spirit seems to be in this man revived."[86] Indeed, three years after the publication of Eaton's *Honey-Combe of Free Justification* (1642), Saltmarsh published his *Free Grace: or, The Flowings of Christ's Blood Freely to Sinners*.

Urged on by what he regarded as the crucial desirability for true justice and righteousness among the people of England, Saltmarsh strove relentlessly to achieve that objective. With William Dell, he preached, and earnestly believed in, the possibility of the fulfillment of that hope through the New Model Army, which he evidently saw as God's instrument to that end. For example, in his "Letter from the Army, Concerning the peaceable temper of the same," Saltmarsh declares: "There is a mighty spirit raised up in the Army for Justice and Righteousness; and we admire at it."[87] A few months later (on Oc-

---

86. *Antinomianism Discovered and Confuted* (London, 1652), p. 35.
87. John Saltmarsh, "A Letter from the Army, Concerning the peaceable temper of the same" (1647), p.2.

tober 28, 1647), Saltmarsh began his "Letter to the Council of War" by reminding the honorable gentlemen about "the sad outcries of a poor nation for justice and righteousness,"[88] and proceeded to accuse them of neglecting their responsibilities to the people:

> But this I know: ye have not discharged yourselves to the people in such things as they justly expected from ye, and for which ye had that spirit of righteousness first put upon ye by an Almighty Power, and which carried you on a conquering wing. *The wisdom of the flesh hath deceived and enticed, and that glorious principle of Christian liberty which we advanced in at first . . . hath been managed too much in the flesh.*[89]

Saltmarsh was convinced that the enticement and deception of "the wisdom of the flesh" had undermined "that glorious principle of Christian liberty which we advanced in at first." To him, the two concerns simply did not belong together. As he insisted in *Some Drops of the Viall* (1646), he could not take his "discoveries of Christ from Reason, nor seek the glory of Him in Forms so much below Him." Consequently, one should earnestly strive, Saltmarsh believed, to free oneself from "vaine Philosophie" and from "the wisdom of the Greek."[90]

Admittedly, Saltmarsh believed with Ralph Cudworth and the other Cambridge Platonists that "the way to heaven is plain and easy, if we have but honest hearts."[91] For Saltmarsh, salvation was "plain, easy, and simply revealed" to all men, including the simplest and meanest.[92] However, Schenk cor-

88. See Woodhouse, p. 438.
89. *Ibid.*; italics mine.
90. P. 115.
91. Ralph Cudworth, *A Sermon Preached before the Honourable House of Commons*, March 31, 1647. Cf. W. Schenk, *The Concern for Social Justice in the Puritan Revolution* (London, New York, Toronto: Longmans, Green and Company, 1948), p. 84.
92. John Saltmarsh, *Sparkles of Glory; or, Some Beams of the Morning Star* (1647), p. 44. Cf. Schenk, p. 86.

rectly concludes that Saltmarsh's fundamental idea can hardly be regarded as celebrating, with John Hales and the members of the Cambridge Platonist School, the significant concept of the "candle of the Lord" or *recta ratio* (right reason) as an important element in men's restoration from sin. As Schenk correctly argues, "the answer cannot be in doubt: Saltmarsh despised human reason and rejected humanism."[93] For a resounding reaffirmation of God's justice, in terms of a viable conjunction of men's reason and faith, we must turn to John Goodwin, to the Cambridge Platonists, and to John Milton.

iii

William Haller suggests that if John Goodwin had not relinquished his fellowship at Queen's in 1627, "possibly he and not Whichcote [to whom Goodwin dedicated his *Redemption Redeemed*, 1651], who had just enrolled at Emmanuel, would have been remembered as the earliest of the Cambridge Platonists."[94] Haller further suggests that "no one represented more clearly [than John Goodwin] the influence of Christian humanism in its Protestant phase upon the Puritan revolutionary movement."[95] Haller's accolades to Goodwin are not misplaced. Indeed, in seventeenth-century Puritanism, John Goodwin (along with the Cambridge Platonists) comes the closest to Milton's understanding of God's justice as essentially creative and restorative, though also potentially damning, depending on one's response to God's offered enlightenment.

To Goodwin, the human faculties of reason and will are the gift of God Himself, who encourages men, by the very nature of the revelation of His truth, to make the fullest possible use

---

93. Schenk, p. 86.
94. Haller, p. 147.
95. *Ibid.*, p. 76.

of these divinely bestowed instruments for their spiritual nurture and growth. For example, in his *Divine Authority of the Scriptures Asserted* (1648), Goodwin insists that

> the true and proper *foundation of Christian Religion* is not inke and paper, not any book, or books, not any writing, or writings whatsoever, whether *Translations*, or *Originalls;* but that substance of matter, those gracious counsells of God concerning the salvation of the world by Jesus Christ, which indeed are represented, and declared, both in Translations, and Originalls, but are essentially and really distinct from both, and no waies, for their natures and beings, depending on either of them.[96]

Goodwin's progressive view of Scripture and its revelation of God's ways clearly transcends the narrow orthodox and moderate Puritan views with their emphasis on the indispensability of "the written law of God."[97] Goodwin does see the Scripture as the Word of God, but it is the Word of God given to men in a manner that requires their vigilant exercise of right reason. For Goodwin, it is *recta ratio*, this important gift of God to men, that makes the progressive discovery of truth both possible for men and sanctioned by God. Goodwin firmly believes that truth, which exists to be discovered by reason, is like "a jewell which lyes out of sight, as it were, in the bowels of many reasons, men must search for it, that wil find it out."[98] Moreover, men must expect that in the very search for Truth, new truths will replace old habits and established customs. Thus, Goodwin decries the "commotions, tumults, and combustions" of those men who balk at the appearance of any truth that threatens to

---

96. P. [17]. Cf. Haller, p. 253.
97. See, for example, section ii above.
98. John Goodwin, *Certain briefe Observations and Antiquaeries: on Master Prin's Twelve Questions about Church-government* (London, 1644), p. 1. Cf. Haller, p. 147.

rack them from off the lees of their old customes, or compell them to restitution of what they have unjustly taken, and peaceably injoyed for a long time . . . what appealings to fire, sword, prisons, banishment, confiscations, and all to turn a beam of light and glorie, into darknes & shame, to keep a new-born Truth from ruling over them.[99]

It is, Goodwin insists, precisely such frantic scurrying away from God's offered enlightenment, such evading of our responsibilities as rational creatures, that brings upon us God's "just severity and indignation." As Goodwin puts it, "when men shall turn their backs upon that 'candle of the Lord' . . . which by the hand of Christ is lighted in every man's soul," God "suspends the influence of his former blessing" and "curseth that tree of light within them," and He does so "in process of his most just severity and indignation."[100] Goodwin's affinity with the Cambridge Platonists is partly indicated here by his use of the phrase "candle of the Lord." Significantly also, he clearly links *with Christ* the only two available alternatives in one's relationship to God. It is Christ who instrumentally sets aflame the "tree of light," a complex symbol of growth and potential darkness—underscored with an implied responsibility for continuous vigilance and care.

Yet, Goodwin's implied concept of divine justice, though closer to Milton's than that of the orthodox and the moderate Puritans of the seventeenth century, cannot be fully identified with Milton's concept of God's justice for an important reason: Goodwin fails to appreciate the full significance of Christ's person and function as God's justice or righteousness. For Milton, Christ is the sole, efficacious means of men's salvation,

99. John Goodwin, *Innocency and Truth Triumphing together* (London, 1645), Epistle. Cf. Haller, pp. 251–52.

100. *The Divine Authority of the Scriptures Asserted* (London, 1648), sig. a2. Quoted in Arthur E. Barker, *Milton and the Puritan Dilemma: 1641–1660* (Toronto and London: University of Toronto Press, 1942; reprinted 1964), pp. 312–13.

through their faith in His meritorious sacrifice to save them (cf. *Paradise Lost* XII, 395-410, e.g.). Goodwin, on the other hand, evidently cannot accept either the biblical truth that the *only* perfect righteousness is the righteousness of Christ or the indispensable concept of Christ's fulfillment of the Law. Regarding the first, Goodwin, as Haller reminds us, "had incurred disapproval for the notions concerning justification expressed in his *Imputatio Fidei* in January, 1642."[101] What Goodwin said about justification in his *Imputatio Fidei* was, among other things, that

that perfect righteousnesse wherein Justification consists, and wherewith men are made formally righteous when they are justified, is nothing else but the remission of sinnes.[102]

In connection with the second, Goodwin rejects the idea of the imputation of Christ's righteousness to us—on the grounds that such imputation would make our justification to be by works of the Law, since Christ fulfilled the Law. The speciousness of Goodwin's point is clear.

Like John Goodwin, the Cambridge Platonists shared with Milton a primary interest in the enhancement of the whole man on the basis of a viable conjunction of reason and faith. Convinced, as Benjamin Whichcote (1610–1683) insisted, that reason was "the very voice of God,"[103] the Cambridge Platonists believed that any deprecation of reason would be "to go against God."[104] But by *reason*, Whichcote and the other members of the Cambridge Platonist School meant *recta ratio*

101. Haller, p. 76.
102. *Imputatio Fidei*. Or "A Treatise of Justification wherein ye imputation of faith for righteousness . . . is explained & also yt great Question largely handled, Whether ye active obedience of Christ performed to ye morall law, be imputed in Justification, or noe" (London, 1642), p. 212.
103. Benjamin Whichcote, *Moral and Religious Aphorisms* (London, 1930; first published 1703), p. 76.
104. *Ibid.*

(right reason), a concept articulated by John Hales (1584–1656). Intensely disturbed by the theological disputes of his day, Hales insisted on defining the practical effect of true religion as "the unity of the Spirit in the bond of peace" (Eph. 4:3). To Hales, moreover, that "Spirit" "is nothing but reason illuminated by revelation out of the written word." [105] It was this understanding of reason that the Cambridge Platonists adopted.

For example, to Whichcote the soul of man was kindled from within by the Spirit, which was "the candle of the Lord lighted by God, and lighting man to God";[106] and John Smith (1618–1652), in his "Discourse concerning the True Way or Method of attaining to Divine Knowledge," urged that

> as the eye cannot behold the sun unless it be sunlike . . ., so neither can the soul of man behold God . . ., unless it be God-like, hath God formed in it, and be made partaker of the Divine Nature.[107]

In fact, unless the soul were kindled by God, all religion was just empty talk, Smith insisted, "a Doctrine that is wrapt up in Ink and Paper." [108] What was required instead was, as William Chillingworth (who, with John Hales, was part of the scholarly gathering which met frequently at the home of Lord Falkland) observed,

> right reason, grounded on divine revelation and common notions written by God in the hearts of all men, and deducing according to the never-failing rules of logic, consequent deductions from them.[109]

Moderate Nonconformists in their relationship to

---

105. "A Tract on . . . the Lord's Supper, " *Works* (1765), 1: 69.
106. See Schenk, p. 84.
107. *Select Discourses* (1660), pp. 2–3. See Schenk, p. 84.
108. *Ibid.*, p. 323. See Schenk, p. 84.
109. *The Religion of Protestants a Safe Way to Salvation* (1638) in *Works* (1838), 1: 14.

seventeenth-century Puritanism, the Cambridge Platonists refused, as did Milton, to accept either the Calvinist concept of
predestination or its motivating doctrinal tenets of obedience
to the Absolute Will of God and the irreparable depravity of
human nature. As Ralph Cudworth pointed out in a sermon
before the House of Commons on March 31, 1647,

> God is . . . God because he is the highest and most perfect
> Good; and good is not . . . good because God out of an
> arbitrary will of his would have it so.[110]

Rather, as Cudworth further explains, men should seek to
know God's purposes for them in their hearts and not "in
those hidden Records of Eternity."[111] Only then will they set
themselves on the right path to achieving happiness, which is
"nothing but that inward sweet delight that will arise from the
harmonious agreement between our wills and God's will."[112]
Primarily concerned with the enrichment of human life
rather than with controversial questions of doctrine, the Cambridge Platonists firmly believed, as Whichcote observes in his
Moral and Religious Aphorisms, that

> the practice of religion is the true use of those faculties with
> which God hath invested human nature.[113]

Such an essentially humanist perspective Milton could, and
did, share. However, as in the case of his theological affinity
with John Goodwin, in the case of the Cambridge Platonists as
well, Milton surpassed the boundaries of even such a vibrant
Christian humanism. For the viewpoint of these learned men,
however enlightened, represented only one strand of Milton's
own complex vision—at the center of which stood the

---

110. Cudworth, pp. 26–27.
111. *Ibid.*, p.11.
112. *Ibid.*, p. 19.
113. Whichcote, p. 983.

sovereign presence of the biblical Christ, the perfect righteousness of God. With that presence and with that sovereignty the members of the Cambridge Platonist School could not fully identify.

In his introductory note to *Paradise Lost*, Frank Allen Patterson cogently argues that "Milton was not a Puritan. Only in the sense that he lived in an age when English policies were dominated by Puritan leaders can he be called a Puritan."[114] Regarding Milton's relationship to seventeenth-century Puritanism, nothing could be more accurate. At least two of the ten major differences that Patterson cites between Milton and seventeenth-century Puritanism stand out (in regard to God's justice) with a compelling significance: Milton's belief in "a world of growth and change" and in "the utmost freedom of the human will."[115]

Even as early as 1644, the thirty-six year old author of *Areopagitica* was convinced of both of these essentially Christian humanist concerns, as his observations on *reason* (the "freedom to choose") and *truth* ("compared in scripture to a streaming fountain") abundantly make clear. In connection with the first, Milton declares:

> If every action which is good or evil in man at ripe years, were to be under pittance and prescription and compulsion, what were virtue but a name, what praise could be then due to well-doing, what gramercy to be sober, just, or continent?
>
> Many there be that complain of divine providence for suffering Adam to transgress. Foolish tongues! *when God gave him reason, he gave him freedom to choose, for reason is but choosing;* he had been else a mere artificial Adam, such an Adam as he is in the motions.[116]

114. Frank Allen Patterson, ed. *The Student's Milton* (New York: Appleton-Century-Crofts, Inc., 1961; first published 1930), "Notes on the Poetry," p. 74.
115. *Ibid.*
116. Merritt Y. Hughes, *John Milton: Complete Poems and Major Prose* (New York: The Odyssey Press, 1957), p. 733; italics mine.

In connection with the second, Milton observes that "truth is strong, next to the Almighty. She needs no policies, nor stratagems, nor licensings to make her victorious. . . . Give her but room, and do not bind her when she sleeps, for then she speaks not true."[117] In fact, no one has, or can have, the whole truth. "Truth indeed came once into the world with her divine Master, and was a perfect shape most glorious to look on." However, "a wicked race of deceivers" subsequently so prostituted her that she became dismembered into a thousand pieces. "We have not yet found them all, Lords and Commons," Milton pleads, "nor ever shall do, till her Master's second coming."[118] Consequently, Milton is totally opposed to any stationary world of dogmatic belief, with pretensions to possessing the whole truth. For Milton, "our faith and knowledge thrives by exercise, as well as our limbs and complexion." Thus,

> Truth is compared in scripture to a streaming fountain; if her waters flow not in a perpetual progression, they sicken into a muddy pool of conformity and tradition.[119]

It was seventeenth-century Puritanism's "muddy pool of conformity and tradition" against which Milton, as Patterson observes, "fought with his whole strength all his life."[120]

Milton's belief in "a world of growth and change" and in "the utmost freedom of the human will" logically leads him to the significant recognition of the true meaning of God's restoration of man from the effects of the Fall. For Milton, the true meaning of God's restoration must be understood, above everything else, in terms of a continuing renewal, to their state of "primitive brightness," of man's natural faculties of reason

---

117. *Ibid.*, p. 747.
118. *Ibid.*, pp. 741–42.
119. *Ibid.*, p. 739.
120. Patterson, p. 74.

and will.[121] As he explains in his discussion of regeneration, the change that is effected in man through the Word of God and the Holy Spirit is a change "in all the faculties of his mind,"[122] which means, Milton points out, "in understanding and will." Further, such a renewal of the will "can mean nothing," Milton argues, "but a restoration to its former liberty"[123]—or, as he puts it in discussing the *law of nature*, that elusive theological concept in Puritanism's view of the nature of man and his relationship to God, a daily movement toward "a renewal of its primitive brightness."[124]

Clearly, such a renewal even in the regenerate holds no guarantee of their ultimate salvation. Even for the elect, Milton believes, there can be no absolute assurance of salvation apart from their continuously vigilant exercise of reason and will as part of their positive response to their election by God.[125] For Milton, it is not the elect, but those who persevere to the end, who will obtain salvation.[126]

Milton's view of the elect and his interest in the renewal of the natural faculties in the regenerate, as well as his basic belief in "a world of growth and change" and in "the utmost freedom of the human will, " all find their full, coherent expression in an aspect of his theology that is far too often avoided, his discussion of predestination in *De Doctrina Christiana*. That Milton firmly believed in predestination there can be no doubt. However, that that belief consequently aligned him with the orthodox and moderate Puritans of the seventeenth century is as preposterous as it is inaccurate. For Milton,

that reprobation, the consequence of which is punishment,

---

121. See Milton's discussion in *De Doctrina Christiana* of "Man's Renovation, including his Calling" and of "Regeneration" in Patterson, pp. 1013–15.
122. *De Doctrina Christiana*, Book I, chapter 18 (Patterson, pp. 1014–15).
123. Patterson, p. 1015.
124. *De Doctrina Christiana*, Book I, chapter 26 (Patterson, p. 1024).
125. See Patterson, p. 1021.
126. See *ibid.*, p. 1022.

> *may be reconciled with justice,* it *must be owing to man's sin alone,
> and not to the arbitrary will of God.* . . . God does not repro-
> bate for one cause, and condemn or assign to death for
> another, according to the distinction commonly made; but
> those whom he condemned on account of sin, he has also
> reprobated on account of sin, as in time, so from all eter-
> nity. *And this reprobation lies not so much in the divine will, as in
> the obstinacy of their own minds; it is not God who decrees it, but
> the reprobate themselves who determine on refusing to repent while
> it is in their power.* [127]

Clearly, not only is there no notion here of a double predestination, but Milton plainly establishes the *reason* why there is
not: "that reprobation . . . may be reconciled with justice."
Nor does Milton evade the issue of "sufficient grace" even for
the reprobate. Not only does he clearly explain that "this
reprobation lies not so much in the divine will, as in the obsti-
nacy of their own minds," but he also insists that

> it is owing to his justice that there are none to whom he
> [God] does not vouchsafe grace sufficient for their salva-
> tion. [128]

For one thing, Milton points out, God "must also will that an
adequate proportion of saving grace shall be withholden from
no man; for if otherwise, it does not appear how his truth
towards mankind can be justified." [129] To put it another way,
orthodox and moderate Puritanism, with their Calvinist insistence on God's double will and on His unconditional and
absolute predestination of some men to election and others to
reprobation, creates in God's ways an irreparable "credibility
gap"—to use our modern jargon—which hardly does credit
to His unimpeachable justice.

Milton is (in keeping with his belief in "a world of growth

---

127. *De Doctrina Christiana,* Book I, chapter 4 (Hughes, p. 928); italics mine.
128. Hughes, p. 926.
129. *Ibid.,* p. 927.

and change" and in "the utmost freedom of the human will")
adamant about this significant point. For if, he argues,

> the condition whereon the decree depends, that is to say, *the*
> *will enfranchised by God himself,* and faith which is required of
> mankind be left in the power of beings who are free agents,
> there is nothing in the doctrine *either derogatory to grace, or*
> *inconsistent with justice,* since the power of willing and believ-
> ing is either the gift of God, or, so far as it is inherent in
> man, partakes not of the nature of merit or of good works,
> *but only of a natural faculty.* [130]

Milton's argument is cogent and places him neither in the
camp of the Calvinists nor in that of the Roman Catholics, but
unequivocally in that small circle of Christian humanists who
illumined an otherwise pedantic and fundamentalist seventeenth-century theological milieu. Significantly, even in his
discussion of the biblically established teaching of predestination, Milton refuses to denigrate either the natural faculties, with their inherent freedom for responsible growth
"under the influence of the Holy Spirit," or the fundamental
integrity of God's justice, with its characteristic quality of
creative and restorative concern.

Milton bluntly repudiates "the scholastic distinction which
ascribes a two-fold will to God; his revealed will, whereby he
prescribes the way in which he desires us to act, and his
hidden will, whereby he decrees that we shall never so act."[131]
To Milton, this is a dangerous piece of folly that impugns the
justice of God:

> Neither in his mode of dealing with our common father
> Adam, nor with those whom he calls and invites to accept of
> grace, can God be charged with commanding righteous-
> ness, while he decrees our disobedience to the command.

---

130. *Ibid.,* p. 925; italics mine.
131. *Ibid.,* p. 919.

*What can be imagined more absurd than a necessity which does
not necessitate, and a will without volition?*[132]

But Milton willingly discards also those tendencies (as demonstrated by John Goodwin and the Cambridge Platonists)
which exaggerate humanistic concerns above the significant
presence and function of the biblical Christ. For at the center
of his understanding of predestination, as indeed at the heart
of his entire theological system, stands the Christ, the merciful, loving, gracious, and wise Justice of God. As he decisively
observes concerning "the chief end of predestination,"[133]

> there was no grace decreed for man who was to fall, no
> mode of reconciliation with God, *independently of the fore-
> known sacrifice of Christ;* and since God has so plainly declared
> that predestination is the *effect* of his mercy, and love, and
> grace, and wisdom in Christ, *it is to these qualities that we
> ought to attribute it, and not, as is generally done, to his absolute
> and secret will.* [134]

Thus, in a special sense, Milton stands, in the seventeenth
century, alone. The reason may well be that, in the final
analysis, Milton is, as J. H. Sims has called him, "a Biblical
poet."[135] The following chapter examines the extent to which
such a claim is true.

---

132. *Ibid.*, italics mine.
133. *Ibid.*, p. 918.
134. *Ibid.*, p. 919; italics mine.
135. James H. Sims, *The Bible in Milton's Epics* (Gainesville, Fla.: University of
Florida Press, 1962), p. 250.

3

Justice and Damnation
in the Biblical Tradition

i

In his recent book *The Ancient Theology*, D. P. Walker observes that during the first few centuries after Christ the Christian tradition (notably through Origen and Augustine) acquired a number of Hellenistic, particularly Platonic, strands.[1] Walker's observation is borne out by several parallels between the works of Plato and patristic thought. For example, in connection with the concept of divine justice as it relates to rewards and punishments in both the present existence and the afterlife, a number of passages in Plato's *Republic*, the *Theaetetus*, the *Laws*, and the *Seventh Letter* indicate the closest similarity to this concept as it developed within the Christian tradition.[2] The fact is that the understanding of divine justice

---

1. (Ithaca, N. Y.: Cornell University Press, 1972), pp. 3–6.
2. For example, in the *Laws* (Book IV), the Athenian stranger, in a pretended speech to recently arrived colonists, declares:

Justice always accompanies him [God], and is the punisher of those who fall short of the divine law. To justice, he who would be happy holds fast and follows in her company with all humility and order; but he who is lifted up with pride, or elated

85

as God's instrument for the punishment of evil goes back to the Hellenistic sense of justice and not essentially to the Old and the New Testaments.

An interesting juxtaposition occurs in the Old Testament between God's justice or righteousness *(zedakah)* and His salvation *(tesuca)*, in which the former is often paralleled, or at least associated, with the latter. This is especially true of Deutero-Isaiah and of the Psalms, in both of which there is a decided emphasis on both the faithfulness of God and His desire to heal or to uphold the people. In Isaiah 45:21, for example, the prophet declares for the Lord:

> there is no God else beside me; a just God and a Saviour; there is none beside me,[3]

and in Psalm 71:15, the psalmist makes a similar association:

> My mouth shall show forth thy righteousness and thy salvation all the day.

In Isaiah 46:12–13, the juxtaposition is even more significant because of the basic meaning of the context in which the words occur:

> Hearken unto me, ye stout-hearted, that are far from righteousness. I bring near my righteousness; it shall not be far off, and my salvation shall not tarry; and I will place salvation in Zion for Israel, my glory.

---

by wealth or rank, or beauty, who is young and foolish, and has a soul hot with insolence . . . is left deserted of God; and being thus deserted, he takes to him others who are like himself, and dances about, throwing all things into confusion, and many think that he is a great man, but in a short time he pays a penalty which justice cannot but approve, and is utterly destroyed, and his family and city with him.

The concept of *distributive* and *retributive* justice, so erroneously overemphasized in the Christian tradition, clearly characterizes this excerpt from Plato.

3. All quotations from the Bible are from the King James Version unless otherwise indicated.

The juxtaposition between the two concepts of God's righteousness and His salvation takes on added meaning when it is associated with the idea of God's judging or of His governing, as is clear from Psalm 67:4 and Isaiah 51:5, to cite only two important examples:

O let the nations be glad and sing for joy, for thou shalt judge the people righteously, and govern the nations upon earth.

My righteousness is near; my salvation is gone forth, and my arms shall judge the people; the isles shall wait upon me, and on my arm shall they trust.

The fact is that in the Old Testament the justice of God is neither essentially *retributive* nor *distributive*, but *restorative*, and is fundamentally based on God's covenantal commitment to Israel. God is just because He is faithful to His promises of salvation and deliverance for the people. Consequently, it is not surprising to find such terms as *justice, salvation, mercy,* and *truth* closely associated, and even used practically interchangeably in the Old Testament. For example, in Psalm 98:2−3, the author declares:

The Lord hath made known his salvation: his righteousness hath he openly showed in the sight of the heathen. He hath remembered his mercy and his truth toward the house of Israel: all the ends of the earth have seen the salvation of our God.

As the *Encyclopedia Judaica* explains,

Jewish justice is different from the classic philosophic (Greek-Western) view of this concept. In the latter, justice is generally considered under the headings of "distributive" and "retributive." These are, of course, also comprised in "zedakah," but while "distributive" and "retributive" justice are essentially procedural principles (i.e., how to do things),

Jewish justice is essentially substantive (i.e., what human life should be like).[4]

This, in the final analysis, is the crucial difference between the Platonic-Augustinian concept of divine justice and the biblical view. In the Bible, divine justice is especially concerned with the enhancement of human life rather than with the forensic or juridical administration of justice or with the concepts of retribution and vengeance. Even where there is a definite emphasis on vengeance, there is usually a similar emphasis on the substantive or restorative nature of divine justice, on the full enrichment of human life.

In Isaiah 59, for example, the prophet presents a vivid account of God's relationship to the people of Israel. The chapter may most conveniently be divided into four basic parts, concerned with (a) the damnable nature of sin; (b) the sins of the people of Israel; (c) the calamity that results from sin; and (d) God's covenantal promise of a Redeemer for the people. Significantly, the chapter begins, as it ends, with a clear emphasis on God's salvation for the people of Israel:

> Behold, the Lord's hand is not shortened, that it cannot save; neither his ear heavy, that it cannot hear. (Isa. 59:1)

Despite the Lord's readiness to hear and to save, however, the sins of the people have made their communion with God impossible. Their hands are defiled with blood and their lips have spoken perverse lies (verse 3); their feet run to evil and their thoughts are thoughts of iniquity (verse 7); they have made their "goings" crooked paths and they do not know the way of peace (verse 8); they multiply their transgressions before the Lord (verse 12) and their speech is totally of oppression and revolt, "conceiving and uttering from the heart words of falsehood" (verse 13). Therefore, the prophet declares:

4. Vol. 10 (New York: The Macmillan Co., 1971): 476.

According to their deeds, accordingly he will repay, fury to his adversaries, recompense to his enemies. (Isa. 59:18)

However, this "recompense" from the Lord is neither essentially because of an inherent sense of upholding His moral will nor basically because of a desire to inflict punishment on the people. It is true that the prophet gives as one reason: "So shall they fear the name of the Lord from the west, and his glory from the rising of the sun" (Isa. 59:19). However, even more prominent is the motivation that precedes the recompense:

And he saw that there was no man, and wondered that there was no intercessor: therefore his arm brought salvation unto him; and his righteousness, it sustained him. For he put on righteousness as a breastplate and an helmet of salvation upon his head; and he put on the garments of vengeance for clothing, and was clad with zeal as a cloke. (Isa. 59:16–17)

Thus, the "recompense" according to their deeds (verse 18) is instrumental to a far more important objective. Equally significant is the fact that the "garments of vengeance" are associated with the breastplate of "righteousness" and the helmet of "salvation."

Further, the qualities of "righteousness" (or justice) and "salvation" (closely associated in this chapter with judgment) are precisely what the people have forsaken through their evil ways and exactly what the "recompense" seeks to restore to them (verses 4; 8–9; 11; and 14–15). Moreover, the positive connotations of "justice" and "judgment" in these verses are not difficult to recognize and make the terms *substantive*, in the sense of their being the desirable objective of the instrumental "recompense" of verse 18, and not *procedural*—which would make "justice" and "judgment" identical with the instrumental "recompense." As a matter of fact, a sense of the desirability of "justice" and "judgment" for the full enhancement of the life of the people so pervades the entire chapter that the reader is hardly surprised at the positive and restorative tone of its concluding verses (Isa. 59:20–21), which unequivocally describe God's covenantal promise of the Redeemer who "shall come to Zion."

However, this restorative emphasis in the concept of God's righteousness is not the exclusive characteristic of divine justice in the Old Testament. With the acceptance of the Deuteronomic code as the ethical canon of the people during the sixth century B.C., the latent concept of God's distributive and retributive justice (always understood to be a part of *zedakah*), together with a consistent emphasis on the individual rather than on the nation as a community, becomes the prominent characteristic of divine justice for the people. The conception of God's righteousness as essentially concerned with blessing and saving the people falls almost totally into abeyance, and "in place of the merciful righteousness of God, we find predominant the distributive, forensic, disinterested righteousness."[5]

The reasonably successful political reorganization of the Jewish nation after the period of the Babylonian captivity (generally understood to have lasted from the conquest of Judah in 586 B.C. to the rebuilding of the temple in 516 B.C.) survived the conquest of Persia by Alexander the Great during the fourth century, and the people seemed basically unaffected politically by the change in suzerainty. In fact, they enjoyed as much freedom under Greece as they had under Persia since the days of Cyrus. Socially and philosophically, however, the impact of Greek domination (which lasted long after the death of Alexander in 323 B.C.) was profound and crucial and the Hebrew religion suffered considerable modification under the tremendous impact of Greek thought and culture.

With the ascension of Antiochus Epiphanes to the Syrian

---

5. W. Bousset, *Religion des Judentums im NT Zeitalter* (Berlin, 1906), p. 436.

throne in 175 B.C., the religious situation deteriorated to
alarming proportions under Antiochus's determination to
eradicate all traces of Jewish faith and practice. In the resulting confusion, innumerable oral interpretations (later to be
developed as the Talmud and the Kabbalah), as well as a spate
of meticulous requirements, were added to the written commandments of the Pentateuch, resulting both in rife sec-
tarianism and in a severe religious legalism. Among the inevitable results of this uncertain process was a seriously reinforced
conception of divine justice as both the exclusive, protective
blessing of the community by a sympathetic God and the
forensic punishment of the individual member of that community who failed to obey the established laws of his God.
This was exactly the situation at the time of the ministry of
Jesus.

In the New Testament, the conception of divine justice is
characterized by both corporate and private, both positive and
negative, both liberating and legalistic, connotations. Moreover, the conception of divine justice in the New Testament
is almost invariably informed by a deep sense of responsibility to reinterpret correctly the meaning of divine justice
(or God's righteousness) in the Old Testament. This is true
not only of St. Paul's definition and discussions of divine justice, but also of Christ's understanding of divine justice as it is
described in the Gospels of Matthew and John.[6]

In Christ's teaching about divine justice, the emphasis is
primarily on one's total commitment to God and a high moral
integrity in one's relationship to others—both the result of a
right understanding of the entire Old Testament. This does
not mean that Christ repudiates the basic significance of the
Law of the Old Testament. Rather, Christ fulfills the Law (cf.
Matt. 5:17), investing the Old Testament concept of God's

---

6. The word "righteousness" ($\delta\iota\kappa\alpha\iota\sigma\sigma\acute{\upsilon}\nu\eta$) occurs only seven times in Matthew,
twice in John, and not at all in Mark and Luke: Matt. 3:15; 5:6; 5:10; 5:20; 6:1; 6:33;
21:32; John 16:8; and 16:10.

righteousness with His own penetrating sense of total commitment not to the letter, but to the spirit, of the Jewish Law. This is the meaning of His whole ministry and message, so aptly summed up in His repetition and interpretation of the significant words of the "Law of Deuteronomy" (Deut. 6:4–5) in Matt. 22:37–40:

> Thou shalt love the Lord thy God with all thy heart, and with all thy soul, and with all thy mind. This is the first and great commandment. And the second is like unto it, Thou shalt love thy neighbour as thyself. On these two commandments hang all the law and the prophets.

Consequently, every occurrence of *dikaiosune* in Matthew and John conveys a basic sense of the Old Testament covenantal relationship, with the indispensable characteristics of God's faithfulness and the people's responsibility. It is in this sense, I suggest, that both Matt. 3:15 and Matt. 21:32, as well as the less difficult allusions to God's righteousness in Matthew and John, must be understood: as a resounding reaffirmation of the fundamental intent, the essential spirit, of "all the law and the prophets."

This incisive look by Christ at the true meaning of "all the law and the prophets" (which pierces its way through the superficialities of a mere legalistic observance—to the core of the Old Testament) is exactly what St. Paul's ministry and message reaffirm. Just as Christ goes back to the core of the Old Testament to reaffirm the essential meaning of God's righteousness, in the same way Paul seeks to discover the true meaning of God's righteousness in a significance much more profound than the mistaken superficial legalism of the Jewish religion. Like Christ, Paul goes back to the Old Testament, but with a notable difference: Paul *explicitly* identifies God's righteousness (*dikaiosune theou*) with Christ Himself. As James

Denney points out, "it cannot be said too strongly that this is the whole of St. Paul's gospel. . . . All the interests of 'righteousness,' in whatever sense the term may be taken, are covered by the δικαιοσύνη θεοῦ which becomes ours through faith in Christ."[7]

For Paul, it is especially in connection with the significance of faith that God's righteousness must be understood. Although Paul goes back, as does Christ, to the core of "all the law and the prophets" (see, e.g., Rom. 13:8,10; Gal. 5:14; and 1 Tim. 1:5), he finds more significance in such Old Testament passages as Gen. 15:6 and Hab. 2:4, with their emphasis on faith, than in those passages where the emphasis is on a kind of automatic salvation for all those who belong to the community of the covenantal arrangements, ratified at Mount Sinai, between God and the people of Israel. Paul bluntly repudiates any emphasis on piety as a result of men's self-achieved righteousness.

Thus Paul combines God's faithfulness in carrying out His promise of salvation with men's unqualified belief in the manifestation of that faithfulness in Christ, the fulfillment of the Law and the Prophets. Consequently, it only through faith, and never through moral or religious observances (however pious and meticulous), that the *dikaiosune theou*, Paul insists, can come to men and become theirs. This is so, Paul argues, because men are, in the last analysis, incapable of fulfilling the Law, since they are incapable of faithfully carrying out the demands of the Law.

This is exactly Paul's point in the *locus classicus* of all his teachings, *Romans 3:20–26*, where the essence of his message concerning the good news of God's righteousness is succinctly presented:

---

7. *Encyclopedia of Religion and Ethics*, ed. James Hastings. vol. 10 (New York: Charles Scribner's Sons, 1961): 789.

Therefore by the deeds of the law there shall no flesh be justified in his sight: *for by the law is the knowledge of sin. But now the righteousness of God without the law is manifested, being witnessed by the law and the prophets.* Even the righteousness of God which is by faith of Jesus Christ unto all and upon all them that believe: for there is no difference. For all have sinned, and come short of the glory of God. Being justified freely by his grace through the redemption that is in Christ Jesus: Whom God hath set forth to be a propitiation through faith in his blood to declare his righteousness for the remission of sins that are past, through the forbearance of God. *To declare, I say, at this time his righteousness: that he might be just, and the justifier of him who believeth in Jesus.* [8]

The *dikaiosune theou* that "without the law is manifested" is, it should be carefully noted, "being witnessed by the law and the prophets." This apparently contradictory point of Paul's is crucial for a correct understanding of divine justice in the Bible. As Paul puts it at the end of this very chapter (Rom. 3:31): "Do we then make void the law through faith? God forbid: yea, we establish the law." Normally understood to mean merely what he asserts in Rom. 3:20, this comment of his, in the context of his point in Rom. 3:21, elucidates Paul's meaning in Rom. 3:26. Paul actually repeats, for emphasis, the phrase "to declare his righteousness" from the preceding verse, adding on this occasion: "at this time." Moreover, Paul is unequivocal about the reason for this declaration by God of His righteousness at this time. There are, in fact, *two* reasons, or at least, a *two-fold* reason: "that he might be just, and the justifier of him who believeth in Jesus."

Evidently, Paul is suggesting that the *dikaiosune theou* is being manifested in Jesus who, because He represents the righteousness of faith, has fulfilled the demands of the Law. However, because He is also the manifestation, "at this time,"

---

8. Italics mine.

of the *dikaiosune theou*, Jesus is the manifestation of God's promise of salvation, articulated for gererations through the Law and the Prophets. Thus, God is "just" in that He has kept His promise, and He is a "justifier" in that He has, at this time, provided the age-old promise, made through the Law and the Prophets, of salvation. However, because Jesus represents the righteousness of faith, that promised salvation now made manifest in Him can become a reality only for "him who believeth in Jesus." Yet, Jesus does not repudiate or abolish, but revalidate or establish, the Law and the Prophets,[9] inasmuch as He demonstrates that God is both "just" and a "justifier."

Consequently, Jesus becomes (however paradoxical it may seem) both the manifestation of God's salvation and the exclusive means through which one may have that salvation. Further, because Jesus revalidates the Law and the Prophets, through which for generations God's righteousness was promised, He simultaneously becomes *that* righteousness, both in the sense of God's mercy and in the sense of God's justice. It is this total conjunction of mercy and justice that Paul has in mind when he declares in this very letter to the Romans:

> For what the law could not do, in that it was weak through the flesh, God sending his own Son in the likeness of sinful flesh, and for sin, condemned sin in the flesh: That the righteousness of the law might be fulfilled in us, who walk not after the flesh, but after the Spirit. (Rom. 8:3–4)[10]

---

9. Cf., e.g., Acts 26:6; Rom. 1:1–2, 15:8; Gal. 4:4–5; and Heb. 1:1–2.

10. Geoffrey Bromiley catches the full meaning of St. Paul's argument when he suggests that

δικαιοσύνη is an expression of grace, but of such a kind that the justice of God is also displayed. . . . We thus have duality, justice and grace being conjoined. . . . From the saving act of the cross Paul gathers assurances of faith that the justice and grace of God are here united for all time and on the deepest level. This means that the antinomian misunderstanding of laxity and feeble compromise is unconditionally excluded. *Forgiveness is an act of judgment in which the justice of God is*

This crucial sense of the two-fold nature of God's righteousness has been largely misunderstood in the developing Christian tradition, with a rather severe bifurcation of the significantly fused nature of God's righteousness into His mercy on the one hand, and His justice on the other—and with a dangerous overemphasis on His justice as distributive and retributive. Beginning with the Judaizing Christians of the early Church (see, for example, Gal. 2:11–16), God's righteousness came to be understood in terms of a strict adherence to moral and religious stipulations set down by the ancient Church. As the Church system developed, this tendency grew more and more predominant, in conformity with the Church's claim of regulative authority over faith and conduct, reinforcing the fallacy of divine punishment as the sole objective of God's justice.

In the Bible, however, the Son of God is not only *like* God's justice; He *is*—as the Covenant tradition clearly illustrates— the justice of God.

ii

St. Paul's clarification of the *dikaiosune theou* pinpoints an important feature in his understanding of God's relationship to men. In his letter to the Galatians, Paul discusses the important issue of the covenant made by God with Abraham. He explains the actualization of God's promises, included in this important covenant, in terms of the manifestation of God's righteousness in Christ. He goes on to argue that the Law, which came much later than God's covenant with Abraham, is

---

fully vindicated. It thus means redemption is sacred purity and with an uncompromising No against evil.

See *Theological Dictionary of the New Testament*, ed. Gerdard Kittel (trans. and ed. Geoffrey W. Bromiley), vol. 2 (Grand Rapids, Mich.: Wm. B. Eerdmans Publishing Company, 1964): 204.

incapable of invalidating the efficacy of that covenant, since the covenant was not only fundamentally one of *promise* and not of forensic propriety, but was also confirmed in Christ (Gal. 3:16–19). Paul's discussion of this covenantal relationship between God and Abraham, in contrast to the characteristic function of the Law, throws into proper perspective the whole question of the meaning of the covenant tradition.

In the Old Testament, the arrangements described by the term "covenant" fall into two categories: first, those in which God communicates to His servants an objective or purpose that He wishes to implement by His own will and power for the benefit of men (as in the case of the covenants with Noah and Abraham [Gen. 8:21–22; 12:1–3]), and second, those in which the conduct of the persons with whom the arrangement is made becomes a determining factor in the implementation of God's promises (as in the case of the covenant at Sinai, and the later covenants with such leaders as Jehoiada, Hezekiah, and Josiah, for example [Deut. 5:1–4, 29–33; 2 Kings 11:17; 2 Chron. 29:10–11; and 2 Kings 23:3]).

In addition to these two basic types of covenants, there is frequent mention by the prophets of a new, spiritual, and everlasting covenant, to be written in the hearts of the people, which God is to establish with redeemed Israel at some future date (for example, Isa. 49:7–8; Jer. 31:31–33; Ezek. 37:26; and Hos. 2:18–20). It is this new covenant that is identified in the New Testament with the good news of the manifestation of God's righteousness and often contrasted with the old covenant of the Mosaic Law (e.g., 2 Cor. 3:5–18 and Heb. 8:6–13). What is especially significant about this new covenant, however, is that it has its prototype in a particular type of Old Testament covenant: in the covenant of promise made by God with Abraham, which Paul discusses in Gal. 3:16–19.

What this means, in effect, is that the *dikaiosune theou* that lies at the heart of Paul's understanding of God's relationship

to men, also lies at the heart of Paul's understanding of the
Covenant tradition. In fact, for Paul, the *dikaiosune theou* is
identified with the new *diatheke* (which is translated in the
Vulgate by the Latin *testamentum*, and in the Authorized Version of the New Testament by the English word *testament*),
and *vice versa*. Consequently, not only can we not define the
one without understanding the crucial import of the other, but
the characteristics of either concept, as far as Paul's entire
theology is concerned, must necessarily be understood as be-
longing to the other as well.

Paul's identification of the *diatheke* with the *dikaiosune theou*
is, however, a most elusive concept, and has been somewhat
responsible for serious difficulties of interpretation in the de-
velopment of what may be called "Covenant Theology." J. S.
Coolidge is quite right when, in his discussion of seventeenth-
century Puritan theology, he observes that

> the Puritan senses strongly the impact of the scriptural con-
> cept of obligation, and in his conviction that a special sense
> of response to God's special will is not 'shut out' by the new
> dispensation he grasps a vital and elusive element in Pauline
> theology.[11]

Coolidge puts his finger on the pulse of the issue, as it has
been demonstrated in the developing stages of Covenant
theology, and W. Adams Brown, suggesting that we may
fairly accurately take Calvin as typical of all the Reformers,
points out the instructive difference between Calvin's and
Irenaeus's views on the nature and the relationship of the two
covenants, the old and the new.[12] Brown explains that Calvin

---

11. John S. Coolidge, *The Pauline Renaissance in England* (London: Oxford University Press, 1970), p. 21.
12. *Encyclopedia of Religion and Ethics*, 4:216. Irenaeus was the only major Patristic
writer to whom the concept of the Covenant seemed worthy of extensive analysis.
Augustine, for example, says nothing about it whatsoever in his major work, *De
Civitate Dei*.

agrees with Irenaeus on the basic use of the term *covenant* for the two dispensations (though not to God's primitive revelation to Adam in Paradise), and that he disagrees with Irenaeus in that Calvin brings both covenants under the conception of grace rather than that of the law. Like the early theologians in general, Irenaeus conceived of God's salvation essentially in terms of the fulfillment of the Law, whereas Calvin, as did all the Reformers, thought of it as a means of rectifying the damage caused by man's transgression of law. Although Irenaeus and Calvin regarded the two covenants as proceeding from the same principle, Irenaeus, in Brown's words, "carries forward the idea of merit from the Law and applies it to the Gospel. Calvin carries back the idea of free grace into the Law, and interprets the latter by the former."[13] And there Brown stops. However, the matter by no means ends there.

Notwithstanding the fundamental difference in their understanding of the "movement" between the two dispensations, both Calvin and Irenaeus confuse the crucial distinction between the Covenant of Grace and the Covenant of Works—an error that St. Paul, for example, painstakingly avoids. Paul expresses the matter most effectively in his letter to the Galatians, which may well be called the Christian's "Declaration of Independence" from the bondage of the Law:

> Stand fast therefore in the liberty wherewith Christ hath made us free, and be not entangled again with the yoke of bondage. . . . For in Jesus Christ neither circumcision availeth anything, nor uncircumcision; but faith which worketh by love. (Gal. 5:1,6)[14]

Irenaeus, by investing the freedom of the Gospel with the burdensome "works-righteousness" of the Law, and Calvin,

---

13. *Encyclopedia of Religion and Ethics*, 4:219.
14. Cf. Rom. 8:15: "For ye have not received the spirit of bondage again to fear; but ye have received the Spirit of adoption, whereby we cry, Abba, Father."

by vainly seeking to define the severe legalism of the Law in terms identical with the liberty of the Gospel, would both inadvertently lead men away from "the liberty wherewith Christ hath made us free." Moreover, although it is not difficult to understand Calvin's basic intention of upholding the sovereign Will of God, it is, nevertheless, easy also to see the danger inherent in a perspective that insists that "when the whole Law is spoken of, the gospel differs from it only in respect of clearness of manifestation."[15] Calvin, like Luther to some extent, firmly believed in one's total submission to the Will of God simply because it was God's Will, and despite their subscription to the fundamental Protestant principle of Christian liberty, they failed to appreciate the full significance of Paul's conviction.

The evident intention of the Reformers, no less than that of Irenaeus, was to guard against all types of antinomianism by insisting on the inescapable responsibility that must accompany the Christian's freedom in Christ. For they understood what Coolidge has admirably articulated in his observation that "Christian liberty is not simply release; rather, it is an active engagement in a struggle like that of organic life to resist dissolution."[16] However, whether this "dynamic of liberty,"[17] as Coolidge aptly calls it, is intended to express the important concept of *simul justus et peccator* (both saint and sinner) or merely the progressive movement of all of Creation toward God's final eschatological revelation, God's *word* in Christ is still "Amen" (2 Cor. 1:20), never again to be either "nay, nay" (2 Cor. 1:17) or even "yea and nay" (2 Cor. 1:18). For the great endorsement that comes with His "yea" and His "Amen" brings with it an uncompromising efficacy against which Law

---

15. *Institutes of the Christian Religion* (II. ix. 4), trans. H. Beveridge (Edinburg, 1875).
16. Coolidge, pp. 39–40.
17. *Ibid.*, p. 40.

and Gospel, bond and free, faithless and faithful alike stand judged.

Moreover, such is the case because that endorsement is the unequivocal fulfillment of "all the promises of God in him" (2 Cor. 1:20), and consequently also, of the *dikaiosune theou*, which not merely includes, but is, the *justice* (or, if you will, the judgement) of God on all His creatures. Consequently, where the response to Christ is positive, this judgment of God brings the activity of the creature to full perfection. However, where the creature's response is negative, persistently resisting and rejecting the attraction of God's grace, that judgment brings a corresponding hardening of the heart, which itself becomes a kind of prelude to a self-imposed fixity in sin, or, as it has been appropriately expressed, to "the final curse of a freely chosen damnation."[18]

The juxtaposition here of "curse" and "damnation" instructively points to the *dikaiosune theou*, the vital link between the two terms, or more accurately, between the two states. For this vital link is not merely the creature's basic freedom of choice (although it surely does include such freedom of decision), but the standard by which all response to the manifestation of the *dikaiosune theou* is to be measured, the *dikaiosune theou* itself. As Coolidge puts it, "the reprobate reject the Covenant of Grace and so are condemned by its condition, 'Whosoever believeth not shall be damned'; or, to put it another way, they come under the Covenant of Works, which automatically condemns them."[19] It is in this sense that the words "freely chosen damnation" should be understood.

The key to this particular aspect of the *dikaiosune theou* may be found in St. Paul's explanation in his letter to the Galatians (3:10–13) that, as he puts it,

---

18. *New Catholic Encyclopedia*, vol. 4, ed. The Catholic University of America (New York: McGraw-Hill Book Co., 1967): 547.
19. Coolidge, p. 116.

> as many as are of the works of the law are under the curse:
> for it is written, Cursed is every one that continueth not in
> all things which are written in the book of the law to do
> them. . . . [But] Christ hath redeemed us from the curse of
> the law, being made a curse for us: for it is written, Cursed
> is every one that hangeth on a tree.

It is in this sense of the inherently cursed nature of the Law,
with its potential ability to inflict its cursed nature on "as
many as are of the works of the law," that damnation ought to
be understood, and not primarily in the sense of God's retributive justice. For it is disbelief in the manifestation of
God's righteousness (that is, in Christ) and His power to re-
deem us from "the curse of the law," that brings upon the man
who so chooses that "curse of the law." Christ's fulfillment of
the Law through His willingness to endure the curses of the
Law liberates us, Paul is arguing here, from those very curses
of the Law—that is to say, from the curse of the old covenant.

In Matt. 25:41–46, Christ's words bring the entire matter to
a critical focus, fusing the formal nature of the curse with its
dialectical significance, as Paul, for example, understands it.
Worded as it is (in verse 41, for instance), Christ's assertion
calls ready attention to the nature of, rather than to the reason
for, the indicated punishment. We should, however, be careful not to separate the one from the other, for the *nature* of the
indicated punishment, however severe and repulsive, is directly dependent on the *reason* for that punishment, and logically calls attention to the equal seriousness and repugnance of
that reason. The reason is, of course, that they are already
cursed—both formally (as verse 41 indicates) and dialectically
(as verses 42–45 illustrate). And the dialectical nature of the
curse is exemplified in their failure to minister, in love, to their
neighbor, or, to put it another way, in their failure to appreciate the meaning of the new covenant, which can be actualized only through a total commitment to Christ, the em-

bodiment of that new covenant. Such a commitment, in turn, must seek to express itself in total love for, and in service to, one's fellowman.

This is exactly Paul's meaning when, in his letter to the Galatians, he declares:

> For, brethren, ye have been called unto liberty; only use not your liberty for an occasion to the flesh, but by love serve one another. For all the law is fulfilled in one word, even in this, Thou shalt love thy neighbor as thyself. (Gal. 5:13 – 14)[20]

Paul conceives of a failure to serve one's neighbor "by love" as a misuse of one's liberty. And Paul can logically make this connection between one's liberty and one's loving service to others because, for Paul, this is exactly what the Gospel is all about, and anything else is necessarily an aberration. Hence,

---

20. St. Paul's argument regarding the Christian's dialectical implementation of his emancipation in Christ has often been misunderstood and/or misrepresented by a number of supposedly well-informed biblical authorities. The Genevan Bible, for example, erroneously glosses Paul's similar argument in Romans 13:8 ("for he that loveth another hath fulfilled the law") as "He meaneth only the second table" of that Law. Reflecting the basic biblical conservatism of Theodore Beza and John Calvin, whose biblical scholarship underscores much of the polemical marginalia of the 1560 Genevan Bible, the gloss inaccurately implies a dichotomy between the first and the second tables of the Law which, in fact, is not confirmed by the spirit and intent of Paul's theological system. Specifically, in this instance, it fails to appreciate the significance of Rom. 12:1 which introduces the whole final section of Paul's letter.

But more than this, the gloss is characteristic of Calvin's overemphasis on *obedience* to the Will of God, further misconstruing the Christian ethic of love, whose motivation and consummation are inspired by Christ's *total* expression of love for men. In fact, the basic inaccuracy of the gloss is that it misrepresents the true significance of love, which alone fulfills the Law (cf. *Paradise Lost*, XII, 402 – 4). For our failure in either of the two great commandments (Matt. 22:37 – 40) is, in effect, a failure in both. As St. John insists, in the classically explicit chapter on the vital importance of love for our brethren (1 John 4),

> God is love; and he that dwelleth in love dwelleth in God, and God in him. Herein is our love made perfect, that we may have boldness in the day of judgment, because as he is, so are we in this world. There is no fear in love; but perfect love casteth out fear: because fear hath torment. He that feareth is not made perfect in love. (I John 4: 16 – 18)

Paul declares (in Gal. 1:8–9), with a decisiveness similar to Christ's in Matt. 25:41:

> But though we, or an angel from heaven, preach any other gospel unto you than that which we have preached unto you, let him be accursed. As we said before, so say I now again, If any man preach any other gospel unto you than that ye have received, let him be accursed.[21]

Thus, whereas in the Old Testament the emphasis is on the formal nature of the curse,[22] in the New Testament there is a decided shift in emphasis to its dialectical significance—and with good reason. In the New Testament, damnation is not simply a matter of retributive justice, and never a case of vindictiveness by God. Rather, it is the inescapable result of the freely chosen alternative to God's offered liberation from the curse of the old dispensation, of the crucial decision to repudiate the proffered grace of the *dikaiosune theou*. The converse of such damnable renunciation may best be understood in terms of the type of significant benediction, for example, with which St. Paul concludes his letter to the Ephesians:

---

21. Cf. 1 Cor. 16:22, where the curse is invoked against anyone who does not *love* the Lord.

22. The curse was initially understood by the ancient Israelites to have an infallible and magical efficacy in bringing evil on the one cursed—a belief that they shared with the neighboring cultures of the ancient Near East. It was widely felt that a curse would invariably implement itself against the one cursed unless it was counteracted by a blessing of equal magnitude and significance (as in Judges 17:2) or turned back upon its author (as in Psalm 109:17–19). With the passage of time, however, Israel's faith in Yahweh's sovereign power over His creation transformed the curse (formerly thought to possess an independent and infallible efficacy) into an expression of God's justice, which, it was believed, operated only to punish the guilty.

In this same sense, Yahweh was thought to be the guardian of all covenants (Gen. 31:44,49), especially the covenant between Himself and Israel (Deut. 26:16–18). Thus, because the people of Israel had broken their covenantal agreement with Yahweh, they had automatically become liable to suffer all the covenant curses connected with such a violation (Deut. 27:14–26; 28:15–68). The Deuteronomist could only hold out the hope that, should they repent, "the Lord, thy God will put all these curses upon thine enemies, and on them that hate thee, which persecuteth thee" (Deut. 30:7). On the other hand, Jeremiah (Jer. 31:31–34) and Ezekiel (Ezek. 16:62; 34:25), e.g., hold out the more radical promise of an entirely new covenant. In the New Testament, Christ is the manifestation of that new covenant.

Grace be with all them that love our Lord Jesus Christ *in sincerity*. Amen.[23]

A much more important dimension is added to the concept of damnation, however, when its characteristic repudiation of God's grace is analyzed in terms of Christ's pertinent remark regarding blasphemy against the Holy Ghost (Matt. 12:31–32). As Jesus puts it in the parallel passage in Mark (3:28–29):

All sins shall be forgiven unto the sons of men, and blasphemies wherewith soever they shall blaspheme: But he that shall blaspheme against the Holy Ghost hath never forgiveness, but is in danger of eternal damnation.

The tone of decisiveness and finality in these words points as clearly to the full extent of possible damnation as the actual words imply the incomparable enormity connected with such a sin. In terms, therefore, of the similar decisiveness and finality of Christ's words in Matt. 25:41, a parallel is surely indicated between the two passages. Evidently, the "curse" of Matt. 25:41 is virtually identical with the "danger of eternal damnation" of Mark 3:29. As a matter of fact, the two suggested consequences are the same and the circumstances surrounding these consequences are quite similar, and, after careful analysis, the reason for the severe punishment indicated in Matt. 25:41 turns out to be precisely the meaning of blasphemy against the Holy Ghost.

The whole question of the "unforgivable sin" (blasphemy against the Holy Ghost) is well elucidated in the Epistle to the Hebrews, particularly in Heb. 6:4–6 and Heb. 10:26–29. In Heb. 10:26–29, for instance, several important points are

---

23. Italics mine. The phrase *in sincerity* is glossed in some versions of the Bible as "with incorruption," which is a much more accurate rendering of the Greek ἐν ἀφθαρσίᾳ. Cf. Titus 2:7, where the word ἀφθορίαν is translated "uncorruptness" in the King James Version.

being made. If we sin willfully, "after . . . we have received the knowledge of the truth," we cannot hope to escape "judgment and fiery indignation" for a most important reason: "there remaineth no more sacrifice for sins" (Heb. 10:26). Moreover, argues the author, if he who despised the Mosaic Law died without mercy, "of how much sorer punishment, suppose ye, shall he be thought worthy" who has done the following things: (i) "trodden under foot the Son of God"; (ii) "counted the blood of the covenant, wherewith he was sanctified, an unholy thing"; and (iii) "done despite unto the Spirit of grace?" Despite the itemized listing here and the different, stated points of reference (the Son of God, the blood of the covenant, and the Spirit of grace), a close examination reveals a common denominator for all three indicated transgressions: the obviously total disregard of the means necessary to effect the alternative of each of the stated transgressions. That means, also implied in the author's comment that "there remaineth no more sacrifice for sins," is clearly *the final sacrifice for sins*, and therefore the stated transgressions are, in effect, a repudiation of that final sacrifice.

Consequently, not only is each transgression, in itself, sufficiently serious to warrant the equally serious consequence of damnation, but to commit any one of these three transgressions is automatically (because of the common denominator of the final sacrifice for sins) to commit them all. Moreover, to commit any, and thus, automatically to commit all, of these transgressions is automatically to place ourselves in the extremely untenable position of requiring yet another sacrifice for sins. This is the meaning of the words in Heb. 6:6:

> seeing that they crucify to themselves the son of God afresh, and put him to an open shame.

And that, in the final analysis, is the unforgivable sin.

It is this "renewed crucifiixion" of the Son of God that is the proper object of eternal damnation. For it is both a repudiation of the *dikaiosune theou* and everything He stands for and a perversion of the conditions of the Covenant of Grace. It is no wonder that for those who so repudiate and pervert such incomparable gifts, it is impossible "to renew them again unto repentance" (Heb. 6:6). For they are, in fact, committing themselves to an unfortunate exchange of the eternal blessings of the New covenant for the eternal curses of the Old.[24]

It is exactly such a repudiation and perversion, on a cosmic and even more decisive level, that Satan exemplifies in *Paradise Lost*.

---

24. Cf. 2 Peter 2:20–21.

4

Satan and the Justice of God
in *Paradise Lost*

i

G. R. Hamilton suggests that "sin is terrible because it is the revolt against love, not because it is the revolt against sheer power."[1] I agree. And in *Paradise Lost*, Satan's sin is terrible because it is the rebellion against God's love, actualized in the Son, who functions in the entire poem as the indispensable creative and restorative agency for the dissemination of that love in practical and exemplary ways.

Milton's emphasis on this particular characteristic of the Son's person and function in *Paradise Lost* is clear. To take merely one example, the scene of the Council in Heaven in Book III, we find the poet describing the Son, in His very first appearance in the poem, in the unequivocal terms of the Son's primary characteristic:

---

1. Hamilton, p. 35.

> Beyond compare the Son of God was seen
> Most glorious . . .
>   and in his face
> Divine compassion visibly appear'd,
> Love without end, and without measure Grace.
>   (III. 138–42)

In the Son—the poet tells us not much later—"the fullness dwells of love divine" (III. 225), and as the Son completes His offer to give His life for Man's restoration,

>   his meek aspéct
> Silent yet spake, and breath'd immortal love.
>   (III. 266–67)

Then, in their song toward the end of the scene, the angels celebrate the Son's unprecedented offer by ascribing to Him the unique title of "unexampl'd love,"

> Love nowhere to be found less than Divine!
>   (III. 410–11)

Further, the Son expresses this divine love in practical, responsible ways, as the Father observes:

>   So Man, as is most just,
> Shall satisfy for Man, be judg'd and die,
> And dying rise, and rising with him raise
> His Brethren, ransom'd with his own dear life.
> So Heav'nly love shall outdo Hellish hate.
>   (III. 294–98)

Moreover, as the Father continues,

>   because in thee
> Love hath abounded more than Glory abounds,

> Therefore thy Humiliation shall exalt
> With thee thy Manhood also to this Throne.
>
> (III. 311–14)

The Father, by His promised exaltation of the Son and by His recognition of the profound significance of the Son's offer, acknowledges, in effect, that decision as the ultimate and most effective response to the great question that He had posed in III. 213–16.

Yet, in all of this, what is even more significant, and what has not been sufficiently explored before, is the explicit identification of *the love of the Son* with *the justice of God*. For what the Father, in fact, asks in III. 213–16 is whether any of the "Heav'nly Powers" will readily give his life so that Man may live—an act that will not only "pay / The rigid satisfaction, death for death" (III. 211–12), but will also *be* an exemplification of *justice*. And such an act would be just for two reasons. First, it will mean divesting oneself of immortality in order to become mortal—a sacrifice that obviously has to be motivated by a "charity" that is both expensive and precious. And second, it will restore to Man an immortality that he will have destroyed by "mortal crime," a crime that will have made him "unjust," a condition, in turn, from which only one who is "just" can "save" him. The Father's question in His exact words is worth repeating here:

> Say Heav'nly Powers, where shall we find *such love*,
> Which of ye will be mortal to redeem
> Man's mortal crime, *and just the unjust to save*,
> Dwells in all Heaven charity so dear?
>
> (III. 213–16)[2]

In these important lines in *Paradise Lost*, not only does "such

---

2. Italics mine.

love" (1. 213) reinforce the preciousness of the charity that is ambiguously "dear" (1. 216), but that reinforcement underscores the meaning of "just," as does the significant use by the poet of "unjust to save" (1. 215). Read exclusively in juridical terms (as it usually is), the full significance of these lines becomes muddled and the Father's point is all but lost. If, however, we read the Father's words here first in terms of the ambiguity of "charity so dear," and then in terms of their special theological meaning, which Milton (as a competent student of the Scriptures) would no doubt make sure that he retained, then the phrase, *just the unjust to save*—which, incidentally, is an almost direct quotation from 1 Peter 3:18[3]—sets up a rather arresting contrast not only between divinity and humanity, but also between the specific characteristic or condition, in the "just" and the "unjust," of *just*ice (or, if you will, of *just*ification).

The point is that the Son is "just" not only because He agrees to suffer the "rigid satisfaction, death for death," but especially because, as the only volunteer for such an exacting responsibility, He confirms both His function as the indispensable agent of God's justice and His person as that very *justice* of God. Further, if we relate—as an accurate reading of the entire scene appears to require—the person of the Son as God's justice with His obviously primary attribute of "charity" (or love), we emerge from the scene with a perspective that has less to do with an austere, juridical transaction than with the poet's portrayal of the Son as the restorative and re-creative justice of God. This, I am suggesting, is fundamentally what the scene of the Council in Heaven in Book III, if read carefully, conveys. And it is, in part, this decisive meaning of God's justice in *Paradise Lost* that Satan does not understand.

---

3. "For Christ also hath once suffered for sins, *the just for the unjust*, that he might bring us to God . . . ." Significantly, the Greek word translated here as "just"

ii

Satan's failure to understand the true significance either of
the Son or of God's justice in *Paradise Lost* springs from his
perverted view of himself and of his place in the universe of
Milton's poem. This perverted perspective continually forces
him, because of its distortion, to define both the person and
function of the Son and the nature and purpose of God's
justice in equally perverted and distorted terms. Satan knows,
as he inadvertently admits, that

> Orders and Degrees
> Jar not with liberty, but well consist.
>
> (V. 792–93)

However, he does not understand the fundamentally creative
nature of the divine order and therefore defines that order
merely in terms of laws and decrees. Moreover, Satan refuses
to recognize the crucial fact that, as a creature, he is inescapably linked with the divine order—not only in terms of his own
nature, but also in terms of his assigned place in that order.
For such an admission would quickly deflate his carefully nur-
tured megalomania and bring him back to a level of reality
where he would be forced further to admit the truth about the
Son and the justice of God (cf. V. 853–64).[4]

Thus, Satan persists in his dream, fondly pursuing his more
enjoyable delusions of greatness and power and vainly seeking

---

(δίκαιος), with its antonym, "unjust" (ἀδίκων), is exactly the same word for "righteous," with its antonym, "unrighteous." See, for example, 1 John 3:7—"he that
doeth righteousness is righteous, even as he is righteous" (ὁ ποιῶν τὴν δικαιοσύνην
δίκαιός ἐστιν, καθὼς ἐκεῖνος δίκαιός ἐστιν), and 1 Cor. 6:9—"Know ye not
that the unrighteous shall not inherit the kingdom of God?" (ἢ οὐκ οἴδατε, ὅτι,
ἄδικοι θεοῦ βασιλείαν οὐ κληρονομήσουσιν).

4. It is significant that of all the points that Abdiel makes in V. 809–48, the
question of Satan's creation is the one with which Satan is almost exclusively
concerned—a fact, by the way, that chronologically is plausible, but in terms of the
time-scheme of the poem, the reader readily recognizes as specious. For Satan has
already admitted the very fact that he is now denying (cf. IV. 43–44).

15
3

to insulate himself—within his own falsehood and artificiality
—from the realities of the poem's world of which he *knows* he
is a part. The sad result is that he rapidly degenerates from
perversity to perversity, spinning a web of distortions in
which he is aware that he is inextricably caught. Satan
knows (as do all the angels in heaven), but because of his
megalomaniacal ambitions, refuses to recognize, that as the
Father's "image" (V. 784), the Son stands at the very center of
the universe of *Paradise Lost* in direct or indirect relationship to
every creature in the poem's world. Satan's problem is that the
inescapable presence of the Son as the Father's very "image"
stands as a viable and potential indictment against his own
delusions of power. For the Son's decisive presence requires
from him, as it does from all creatures—Satan is well
aware—an equally decisive response, for better or for worse,
for creative growth or for self-destructive stagnation, for restoration or for judgment, for salvation or for damnation. Cling-
ing to his perverted view of the person and function of the Son
and of the nature and purpose of God's justice, Satan chooses
contemptuously to disregard the decisive presence of the Son
of God.

Thus, when the Almighty exalts His Son on one of the
feast-days in Heaven, appointing Him head of all the angelic
Host by an irrevocable decree, Satan abhors the very thought
of yet another set of laws and resolves to revolt, drawing after
him "the third part of Heav'n's Host" (V. 710). Abdiel alone,
"than whom none with more zeal ador'd / The Deity, and
divine commands obey'd" (V. 805–6), resisted Satan's instigation to cast off what Satan has convinced himself is "this Yoke"
(V. 786) of

> prostration vile,
> Too much to one, but double how endur'd,
> To one and to his image now proclaim'd?
> (V. 782–84)

The upshot of Satan's instigation is the three-day War in
Heaven, the end of which finds Satan and his rebellious Host
routed by the terrible wrath of the Father through the Son,
until, in desperate flight,

>   headlong themselves they threw
> Down from the verge of Heav'n, Eternal wrath
> Burn'd after them to the bottomless pit.
>   (VI. 864–66)

It is here, *in medias res*, that the main events of *Paradise Lost*
begin.

To the narrative voice, Satan's rebellion made him, among
other things, an Apostate (see V. 852; VI. 100; VII. 43–44), a
deserter or defector—that is, one who breaks his allegiance or
loyalty to a higher authority. And it is especially in this sense,
I submit, that the poet of *Paradise Lost* conceives of disobedience (see, for example, IX. 261–62; III. 203–4). For Milton,
disobedience (the announced subject of *Paradise Lost* in the
very first line of the poem) is much more than the mere violation of a specific command or decree.[5] As he puts it in the
Father's important second speech in Book III,

>   Man disobeying,
> Disloyal breaks his fealty.
>   (III. 203–4)

But why, then, the Father's specific Decree that exalts the
Son, and the command that "to him shall bow / All knees in
Heav'n, and shall confess him Lord" (V. 607–8)?

---

5. C. F. Allison explains that in the seventeenth century (especially after 1640) the
conception of sin held by most theologians was one of *transgression* rather than of a
condition of *alienation* from which transgressions flourish as symptoms. Allison finds
that John Donne was perhaps the most consistent in describing sin as more than mere
acts of transgression. To Donne, sins are symptoms and expressions of a much deeper
state of sin, which is ultimately a condition of radical alienation (see Allison, pp. 202
and 211–12). Milton appears to have held this same view of sin.

One answer, offered by Balachandra Rajan, is that

there are times when Milton, far from avoiding the confusion of appearances, seems intent on adding to it, perhaps as a test of the reader's vigilance. The prohibition against eating the fruit is in the Bible and cannot be escaped from; but the unexplained exaltation of the Son at the beginning of celestial history is neither in the Bible, nor in tradition, nor in the *De Doctrina,* and is therefore a difficulty which Milton chose to make for himself.[6]

By my reading, however, such an answer is inadequate. Apart from our difficulty in understanding the representation of the acts of a divine being who is omnipotent, omnipresent, and omniscient,[7] the exaltation of the Son "at the beginning of celestial history" is, though not in the Bible, nor in tradition, nor in *De Doctrina,* indispensable to Milton's more significant poetic portrayal both of the Son as the "image" (as Satan admits in V. 784) and as the only-begotten (V. 603–4)[8] of God, and of the Son's vital and decisive relationship to the essentially creative function of God's justice.

It is, for instance, most significant that the Father not only associates the Son with His Decree, but also distinctly associates His Decree and command with the question of obedience and loyalty:

> him who disobeys
> Mee disobeys, breaks union, and that day
> Cast out from God and blessed vision, falls
> Into utter darkness, deep ingulft, his place
> Ordain'd without redemption, without end,
> (V. 611–15)

---

6. *"Paradise Lost:* The Web of Responsibility," *Paradise Lost: A Tercentenary Tribute,* ed. Balachandra Rajan, pp. 122–23.

7. Cf. Cormican, p. 184, where the suggestion is made that Milton often made use of the "telescoping of events" for the special purpose of presenting "the successive working out of what is eternally present in the Divine Mind."

8. Merritt Hughes's explanation of the meaning of *begot* in V. 603 is well taken, and

thereby suggesting, it would appear, a definite purpose for the
Decree and command, in the first place: as a test of obedience
and loyalty. Significant also is the negative form of the
Father's statement ("disobeys"; "breaks union"; "cast out"; and
"falls," for example), further suggesting its presentation to the
angelic Host as a prohibition, and thus—as with that associated with the Fall of the human pair—in association with
the Fall of Satan and his angels. Evidently, Milton knows
precisely what he is doing. What he is doing becomes clearer
not much later as we listen to Satan's misreading (whether
conscious or unwitting matters little here) of the purpose of
the Father's Decree and command (V. 792–99).

Satan does not associate the Decree and command with the
prohibition because, I suggest, he fails to understand the prohibition as a test of the obedience and loyalty of the angelic
Host. Quite apart from his obvious "envy against the Son of
God" (V. 709), Satan sees obedience as vile submission, and
repudiates as inconsequential any command or decree intended to elicit and/or test obedience and loyalty. Milton
makes this quite clear, for instance, on the occasion of Satan's
return to Pandaemonium after his successful campaign against
Adam and Eve. Satan seems almost ecstatic with glee (cf. X.
625–27) as he explains his easy success over the human pair,
poking fun at God, as well as at Adam and Eve, over the
incredible significance they attach to an apple:

> Him by fraud I have seduc'd
> From his Creator, and the more to increase
> Your wonder, with an Apple; he thereat
> Offended, worth your laughter, hath giv'n up
> Both his beloved Man and all his World,
> To Sin and Death a prey, and so to us.
>
> (X. 485–90)

---

does not invalidate the basic point being made here (see Hughes, *John Milton: Complete
Poems and Major Prose*, p. 316n.).

For Milton, however, both the prohibition against Adam and Eve and that against the angels are of the utmost significance, since they both serve as *indispensable* tests. As Milton explains in *De Doctrina Christiana*, God, having placed man in the garden of Eden and given him everything necessary for a happy life, "commanded him, as a test of his obedience, to refrain from eating of the single tree of knowledge of good and evil, under penalty of death if he should disregard the injunction."[9] Milton then continues with the important explanation that

> it was necessary that something should be forbidden or commanded as a test of fidelity, and that an act in its own nature indifferent, in order that man's obedience might be thereby manifested. For since it was the disposition of man to do what was right, as a being naturally good and holy, it was not necessary that he should be bound by the obligation of a covenant to perform that to which he was of himself inclined; nor would he have given any proof of obedience by the performance of works to which he was led by a natural impulse, independently of the divine command.[10]

It is this crucial point which Satan does not understand, as is clear from his question in V. 797–99:

> or can introduce
> Law and Edict on us, *who without law*
> *Err not?*[11]

Satan has no trouble recognizing that, like "other Powers as great" (IV. 63), he had "the same free Will and Power to stand" (IV. 66), and he rues his choice of rebellion against God (IV. 71–72). Beyond that, however, he falls back lamely on

---

9. Book I, chapter 10 (Hughes, p. 993).
10. *Ibid.*
11. Italics mine.

his rationalization about Heaven's injustice and tyranny, completely missing the important point that Raphael explains to Adam concerning both men and angels:

> for how
> Can hearts, not free, *be tri'd whether they serve*
> *Willing or no*, who will but what they must
> By Destiny,
>
> (V. 531–34)[12]

and which the Father reiterates just before the Creation in Book VII:

> till by degrees of merit rais'd
> They open to themselves at length the way
> Up hither, *under long obedience tri'd.*
>
> (VII. 157–59)[13]

The point is that obedience to God is significant both as a *test* by the Creator of the creature and as a *pledge* from the creature to the Creator, a fact that every major character in the poem,[14] except Satan, understands.

iii

Because of his perverted view of the Son as God's justice, and of the whole question of his obedience to God, Satan consistently refuses to respond positively and creatively to all opportunities for his restoration. Even when, on Niphates' top, his "conscience wakes despair / That slumber'd, wakes

---

12. Italics mine.
13. Italics mine.
14. See Adam's words to Michael in XII. 557–64, for instance, and the angel's reply to Adam in XII. 575–82. The Son's entire role in *Paradise Lost* is one of a totally obedient response to the Father's inducing ways, and there is never any doubt about his filial loyalty to God (see III. 264–71, e.g.), or about his belief regarding obedience to God by anyone (VI. 740–41).

the bitter memory / Of what he was, what is, and what must
be / Worse" (IV. 23–26), and prompts him to consider
whether he "could repent and could obtain / By Act of Grace
my former state" (IV. 93–94), he misconstrues repentance as
lame submission (IV. 79–82) and bluntly recommits himself
to a gross perversion of his creative opportunity:

> Evil be thou my Good: by thee at least
> Divided Empire with Heav'n's King I hold
> By thee, and more than half perhaps will reign;
> As Man ere long, and this new World shall know.
>
> (IV. 110–13)

It is interesting to observe that in a similar experience of misery and despair, prompted by his accusing conscience, Adam
readily likens his situation to Satan's, both in motive and in
result, both in terms of his misuse of his God-given opportunities and in terms of the harsh reality of divine justice with
regard to his apostasy (X. 837–44). Few readers will miss the
echo here of the Father's decree in His second speech in Book
III regarding the obstinately perverted use of God-given powers and opportunities (II. 198–202) or of Satan's admission on
Mount Niphates (IV. 93–109).

Satan's recommitment to evil at the end of his soliloquy on
Niphates' top, despite the agonies of his awakened conscience,
underscores the enormity of his perversion and calls attention
to Milton's sophisticated sense of the complexity of satanic
evil. Looked at from this perspective, all notions about Satan
as the hero of *Paradise Lost*, or as the consummate fool of
Milton's epic, ought to be closely reexamined in terms of the
poet's keen awareness of such perversity. Correspondingly,
the source of such perversion and evil ought to be understood
not merely in terms of pride or ambition or self-assertion or
disobedience or any number of partial satanic failings, but
essentially in terms of the whole complex of satanic aberra-

tions that only together can properly define the primary satanic culpability: the obstinate and irreparable distortion of God-given powers and opportunities and the consequent perversion of the creative and restorative processes basic to Satan's true nature and inherent in the world of *Paradise Lost*.

That Satan abuses such powers and opportunities throughout the poem Milton is very careful to make clear—mainly through the parodic mimesis of Satan's career, in contrast to representations of loyalty and of the right use of reason and will by the Son, the unfallen angels, prelapsarian (as well as postlapsarian) Adam and Eve, and the narrative voice itself. However, Milton is equally careful to portray Satan's abuse of his creative potential in clear-cut, straightforward instances, even in sections of *Paradise Lost* where satanic perversity dominates the action and the style of the poem in appropriate parodic patterns.

An important example of this occurs in Book II, at the conclusion of the Council in Pandaemonium, clearly a parody of the Council in Heaven in Book III. During his persuasive speech to the assembled Host of Hell, Beelzebub—Milton tells us—"Pleaded his devilish Counsel, first devis'd / By *Satan*, and in part propos'd" (II. 379–80), that all effort be directed toward an assault on the newly created World and its inhabitants. "With full assent / They vote" (II. 388–89), pleased with the shrewd suggestion. In obvious parodic anticipation of the Father's great question in Book III (11, 213–16), as well as the great silence that follows (III. 217–24), Beelzebub poses much the same question as the Father asks in Book III: "But first whom shall we send / In search of this new world, whom shall we find / Sufficient?" (II. 402–4). Having posed the question, "he sat; and expectation held / His look suspense, awaiting who appear'd / . . . but all sat mute / Pondering the danger with deep thoughts" (II. 417–21). Satan, of course, heroically volunteers, quickly cutting off any last-minute offers now that the danger is passed. The Council, revering him appropriately,

>   bend
> With awful reverence prone; and as a God
> Extol him equal to the highest in Heav'n:
> Nor fail'd they to express how much they prais'd,
> That for the general safety he despis'd
> His own. . . .
>
>   (II. 477–82)

Then Milton adds:

>   for neither do the Spirits damn'd
> Lose all thir virtue.
>
>   (II. 482–83)

    Notwithstanding Satan's shrewd arrangement of much of this event, the fallen angels' homage is obviously sincere, and there is nothing to suggest, despite the highly parodic pattern throughout the scene, that Milton's comment is not. For one thing, the tone of the narrative voice suggests that the poet is providing yet another detail about Satan and his fallen Host. Thus, Satan's sacrifice, if not the method used to put it across, appears perfectly genuine, and is, to a large extent, subsequently confirmed by his hazardous journey up to the new World. More significantly, we ought to note the context of what Milton regards here as *virtue:* one's practical, positive, and creative response in the face of severe and real hazards. This, in fact, is what takes place in the case of the Son's promised sacrifice of himself for man in Book III. Further, both the Son's and Satan's sacrifice confirm, and are confirmed by, Milton's plain definition of true virtue in *Areopagitica,* for example, where he discusses the difference between true virtue and a blank virtue.[15]

One can hardly contend after this that Satan is totally devoid of virtue, or at least of the capacity for virtuous conduct, and the kind of conduct that does not merely submit to authority in contrast to the exercise of one's free will and reason. Satan's problem, to repeat, is not so much that he spurns submission in preference to self-assertion and hazardous confrontation, but that he fails to recognize the essential difference between passive submission (which he calls "subjection" [IV. 50]) and that "submission" which is, in fact, a continuously vigilant, creative, and sometimes even woeful imitation of the divine ways. Satan's commitment is evil not because he is totally incapable of selflessness (we have seen that he is not so totally incapable), but because, though capable of self-fulfillment, in consonance with the creative matrix of the poem's world, he chooses instead to pervert his God-given powers (of reason and will) and opportunities (for positive, creative response).

iv

Satan's perverted view of the Son, of God's justice, of the whole question of his obedience to God, and of his own person and place in the universe of *Paradise Lost* forces him into an inexorable process of degeneration, which, in turn,

> like a devilish Engine back recoils
> Upon himself.
>
> (IV. 17–18)

---

15. See Hughes, pp. 728–29: "As therefore the state of man now is . . . that he might see and know, and yet abstain." Incidentally, there is no single moment in the whole of *Paradise Lost* when Satan is not portrayed as having fallen, or as being in the process of falling, from his loyalty to God.

Thus, although he desperately wishes to escape from the constricting process of his self-imposed damnation, he discovers instead that, as he puts it on Mount Niphates,

> myself am Hell;
> And in the lowest deep a lower deep
> Still threat'ning to devour me opens wide,
> To which the Hell I suffer seems a Heav'n.
>
> (IV. 75–78)

⌈The truth is that, by his obduracy and incorrigibility, Satan has metamorphosed the physical Hell, from which he struggles to be free, into a psychological reality that engulfs his total being in a relentless process of degeneration. For Satan has, by his absolute commitment to Evil, fused the physical and the psychological into an inseparable and damning unity⌋ As Milton observes,

> within him Hell
> He brings, and round about him, nor from Hell
> One step no more than from himself can fly
> By change of place.
>
> (IV. 20–23)

Consequently, whether it is "flaming from th' Ethereal Sky" (I. 45) or "rolling in the fiery Gulf" (I. 52) or "High on a Throne of Royal State" (II. 1) or "on the brink of Hell" (II. 918) or "upon the firm opacous Globe / Of this round World" (III. 418–19) or "on Niphates' top" (III. 742), "within him Hell / He brings" (IV. 20–21). The place or the time makes absolutely no difference, for Satan has committed himself to an obdurate and incorrigible perversion of his God-given reason and will.

That is why—when, at the beginning of Book I, he is tormented not only by "lasting pain" but also by the memory of his "lost happiness" (1. 55), and can still recall "the happy

Realms of Light" (1. 85); can recognize his state of misery (1.
90) and the physical change that has already set in (1. 97); and
can even admit his defeat during the War in Heaven (1.
105)—he still feels compelled to play the role of military
leader (which his megalomania never allows him to abandon
throughout the epic) and sneers at the Almighty "with bold
words" (1. 82), "Vaunting aloud, but rackt with deep despair"
(1. 126). Even when Beelzebub is led by plain logic to ask:
"What can it then avail . . . ?" (I. 153 ff.), Satan, "with
speedy words" (I. 157), reproves his fellow and, still playing
his role, slips from pretense into perversity:

> To do ought good never will be our task,
> But ever to do ill our sole delight,
> As being the contrary to his high will
> Whom we resist.
>
> (I. 159–62)

Throughout the rest of the poem he never changes his mind.
Although he does have a moment of honesty here or a thought
of others there, he never renounces this recommitment to evil.
As he puts it in this very first scene,

> If then his Providence
> Out of our evil seek to bring forth good,
> Our labor must be to pervert that end,
> And out of good still to find means of evil.
>
> (I. 162–65)

With a "like doubtful hue" upon his own countenance as he
calls out to the fallen angels, Satan persists in playing the
dubious role into which he has thrown himself, and thus, "he
his wonted pride / Soon recollecting" (I. 527–28), he plunges
into yet another performance (11. 528–29), virtually lashing
his troops verbally back to consciousness. In his next two
public speeches, his role-playing becomes progressively elabo-

rate, and he even seems convinced of his own specious logic and blatant lies. Yet, surrounding his show-business posture are latent opportunities for restoration, which he, however, perverts, because "the show must go on." He does feel "remorse and passion" (I. 605) at the sight of his "followers," not really "fellows of his crime" (I. 606),

> from Eternal Splendors flung
> For his revolt, yet faithful how they stood,
> Thir Glory wither'd,
>
> (I. 610–12)

a pathetic picture and itself a lesson in the kind of loyalty that his present actions continue to repudiate. And this may well be why he weeps—at least from a sense of the enormity of his crime, if not also here from his "dread of shame / Among the Spirits beneath, whom I seduc'd" (IV. 82–83). At any rate, "in spite of scorn" (I. 619), he weeps, interweaving "with sighs" (I. 621) his determined performance.

The whole question of loyalty is on his mind during his speech at the beginning of Book II, and that is practically all he talks about. Characteristically, his logic is spurious at best, and his speech is, in reality, a piece of deceptive bombast, despite the obvious parodic anticipation of the Father's first speech (both in tone and in content) during the Council in Heaven in Book III. The parody succeeds, however, because Satan is obviously lying, his logic is noticeably twisted, and the reader is not likely to forget his tears (less than two hundred lines before) in connection with the pathetic picture of his seduced followers.

Satan's emphasis on "merit" during his speech subtly reinforces the parodic intent, since the exalted monarch has already had both his "merit" and his "eminence" characterized for us by the poet (II. 5–6), and since, ironically, Satan is forced to plead "merit" while pursuing the pretense of being

monarch by "just right and the fixt Laws of Heav'n" (II. 18).
The parody is further enhanced by the ambiguous comment
"this loss / Thus far at least recover'd (II. 21–22), which, even
if we were willing to pretend ignorance of "the will / And high
permission of all-ruling Heaven" (I. 211–12) as the fundamental reason for Satan's survival and recovery, is, nevertheless,
questionable when used as the basis for an obvious lie: that
Satan now sits on "a safe, unenvied Throne / Yielded with full
consent" (II. 23–24)—a consent that he frantically rushes on
to elicit with a piece of specious logic.

   Further, even if we ignore the poet's comment about Satan's
unfounded hope with which he has evidently become intoxi-
cated, "insatiate to pursue / Vain War with Heav'n" (II. 8–9),
and so ignore as well the vanity of Satan's empty boast: "I give
not Heav'n for lost" (II. 14), Satan's other references to
Heaven would be quite ludicrous but for the fact that what he
says is true, we realize, and no one knows the truth about this
better than Satan, since it was he who both envied his superior
and disturbed Heaven's "firm accord" (II. 36).[16] After all of
this, we can easily recognize Satan's fatuous claim in II.
37–40. However, although we recognize this bombastic claim
as the completion of the parodic pattern here (with a kind of
double parody in which Satan has been imitating both the
Father and the Son), we do not ridicule the speaker because,
however preposterous the claim, we can also recognize it as
the spurious logic of a desperate mind, falsely imitating the
characteristics of the admitted "happier state / In Heav'n" (II.
24–25), because perverting those very creative and restorative
characteristics upon which a true imitation must rest.

   Apart from the vacuous rhetoric that characterizes this
parody at the beginning of Book II, the imagery (with its
central figure of Satan "high on a Throne of Royal State,"

---

16. Cf. Death's accusations in II. 689–90.

aspiring even higher than he should sensibly dare to hope) and the epic style (including the persistent saber-rattling and imperial pronouncements) encourage the impression of Satan as "Hell's dread Emperor with pomp Supreme" (II. 510)—a decided requirement if the scene is to succeed as a parody. In fact, the martial and heroic language and imagery of the entire Council in Pandaemonium seem purposely designed to sustain such an impression, and are considerably reinforced toward the end by Milton's almost solicitous attention to Satan's offer to face alone the trials of the long, hard way "that out of Hell leads up to light" (II. 433); to the devils' "rejoicing in their matchless Chief" (II. 487); to Hell's "Firm concord" (II. 497); to the highly regal conclusion of the Council (II. 504–20); and to the typical epic interlude of the sports of the demons, including their remarkable musical harmony that "Suspended Hell, and took with ravishment / The thronging audience" (II. 554–55), as well as their "discourse more sweet" (II. 555) and "pleasing sorcery" (II. 566).

That Milton consciously manipulates our impression toward the image of Satan as "Hell's dread Emperor with pomp Supreme" should, however, not cause us to overlook either the significant phrase that immediately follows: "And God-like imitated state" (II. 511) or the equally important qualification that precedes it: "and seem'd" (II. 508). Milton carefully encourages such an impression in the rest of the scene of the Council in Pandaemonium, with its typical epic conclusion, because it is important as a foil to the sharp stylistic and thematic change that occurs when Satan encounters Sin and Death at Hell's gate. Just as our impression of Satan as Monarch of Hell is necessary for the success of the parody at the beginning of Book II, such an impression, considerably intensified, is vital as a prerequisite for the conspicuous contrast that it provides with the parody of the infernal trinity. Satan's Godlike, imitated state reaches its height in this parody, with its deflating allegorical style and its reinforcement of the theme of evil. Even more significant, however, are the distorted reflection of God's true light and the perverted abuse of creative relationships that it so effectively illustrates.

At the center of the parody is the birth of Sin, critically characterizing the true nature of evil both as a distorted process of self-love and as a perverted miscarriage of true imitation:

> All on a sudden miserable pain
> Surpris'd thee, dim thine eyes, and dizzy swum
> In darkness, while thy head flames thick and fast
> Threw forth, till on the left side op'ning wide,
> Likest to thee in shape and count'nance bright,
> Then shining heav'nly fair, a Goddess arm'd
> Out of thy head I sprung.
>
> (II. 752–58)

While the specific characteristics of the process here ("Miserable pain," dim eyes, dizziness, and darkness, "flames thick and fast," Sin's springing out of Satan's head, and the similarity of shape and appearance between the father and the daughter) illustrate the results of a perverted love of self and apostasy against God, the process itself appropriately fuses with the allegorical mode that Milton uses here, actualizing the monstrous mental abstraction and aberration that is the inevitable result of distorted imitation (moral or artistic). Further, Milton's implied reference to the myth of the birth of Athena (who is represented as emerging from the head of Zeus in Hesiod's *Theogony* [ll. 925–29]) is a good example of such distorted imitation, in keeping with what appears to be Milton's general attitude in *Paradise Lost* toward the classical myths as imperfect imitations of true occurrences. Milton, in fact, appears to be suggesting that the allegorical Sin is doubly parodic (as a parody of a parody), since she is twice removed from the pattern and substance of Truth, more resembling the similarly allegorical Error of Spenser's *Faerie Queene*.[17]

As Satan's "perfect image" (II. 764), Sin is a parody of the Son of God, who is the "Divine Similitude, / In whose conspicuous count'nance . . . th' Almighty Father shines" (III. 384–86). What is conspicuously different, however, is Satan's narcissistic lusting after his own image (II. 763–67), with the incestuous result of Death's conception in Heaven and birth in Hell. Clearly, Death functions in the scene as the third member of the parodic trinity of Hell. However, "this odious offspring" (II. 781), Satan's "own begotten" (II. 782), functions even more significantly as a reinforcement of Satan's distortion of true imitation, both in terms of the perverted abuse of creative relationships (as Death's "fatal Dart / Made to destroy" [II. 786–87] seems to suggest) and in terms of the distorted reflection of God's true light (as his inherent power to distort and transform [II. 783–85] appears to indicate).

It is particularly in this sense that Milton's poetry in this scene ought to be understood. Thematically, if such powers of distortion and destruction characterize the "Son," they would logically reside as well—and with even more potency—in the "Father," especially when the characteristics of the "Father" have the capability of twice transmitting themselves, first, to the daughter, Sin, and then, through the daughter and wife, to the son and grandson, Death. Stylistically, it is in this respect also that we should see Milton's superb change from epic narrative (involving a multiplicity of "external" dramatic elements) to the allegorical mode (in which the various poetic elements become more than ostensibly symbolic and the literary focus becomes appropriately internal).

---

17. See Merritt Hughes's note on *Paradise Lost*, II. 798, where he suggests, in connection with Death's incestuous rape of his Mother, Sin, that "both the allegory and the details resemble Spenser's Error" (Hughes, p. 25ln.).

V

Milton's portrayal of the infernal trinity in Book II underscores the implications of Satan's involuntary metamorphosis
as a serpent in Book X (ll. 511–15). As Arnold Stein has
suggested, Satan

> is drawn gradually into the mechanical existence of his un-
> willed creations, Sin and Death. It is part of their structural
> role to show this, for their allegorical being constitutes a
> kind of stable measure, but their author changes, to become
> more like his images.[18]

Stein's observation is especially valuable for its emphasis on
Satan's degeneration into the form of "a monster illustrating
an allegory," and in that sense, "cut off from true reality, the
whole imaginative vision of true creation and the true
poem."[19] A serious problem arises, however, when we insist
on linking Satan's eventual mechanistic and allegorical demonstration with what Stein calls "the illusion of dramatic
being."[20] However much Satan is involved finally with allegory, or throughout the poem with patterns of parody, he is
simultaneously, if not tragic, at least dramatic, in terms of his
plain obduracy, which is the result of his own free choice (see
IV. 71–72), the result, in turn, of his "free Will and Power to
stand" (IV. 66). And it is precisely such "free Will and Power
to stand" which, as is true of all of God's creatures, is the
essence of his being.

In Satan's "great assertions of individual will,"[21] it is the
greatness of his assertions, rather than his individual will, that

---

18. See *Milton's Epic Poetry: Essays on Paradise Lost and Paradise Regained*, ed. C. A.
Patrides (London: Penguin Books, 1967), p. 115.
19. *Ibid.*, p. 116.
20. *Ibid.*, p. 115.
21. *Ibid.*

is dramatically illusory. For to remove that essential freedom of will (even after Satan's involuntary metamorphosis) is to change his logical degeneration of character into a contrived degradation by the poet, as A. J. A. Waldock erroneously maintains.[22] It is, further, to disregard (to the disadvantage of the poet and of the entire thematic scheme of *Paradise Lost*) Satan's obstinate commitment to evil even after his equally *involuntary* change "in outward luster," with which the process of both his degeneration and his incorrigibility began (I. 94–98). Merritt Hughes is right that Satan can discover that he himself is Hell "without fading into an abstraction of pure allegory" in his world of evil, "where all things are monstrous reflections of the evil in the hearts of his followers."[23]

Moreover, it is important to remember what is evidently too often forgotten: that Satan and his infernal peers, as Milton distinctly tells us, are permitted to resume their "lost shape" (X. 574),

> Yearly enjoin'd, *some say*, to undergo
> This annual humbling certain number'd days,
> To dash thir pride, and joy for Man seduc't.
> (X. 575–77)[24]

Milton appears to be suggesting that although this is the last scene in which Satan as a character appears, it by no means

22. See, for example, Waldock's discussion of what he calls the "cartoon scene" in Book X, when the intended roar of Satan's peers turns involuntarily into a mammoth hiss (*Paradise Lost and Its Critics* [Cambridge: Cambridge University Press, 1947], pp. 91f.). But see Arnold Stein, "Satan and the Dramatic Role of Evil," *PMLA* 45 (1950): 226 where Stein understands the scene as "an external confirmation (necessary in the drama) of the internal failure."

23. *Ten Perspectives on Milton* (New Haven, Conn.: Yale University Press, 1965), p. 164.

24. Italics mine. The phrase *some say* appears to suggest that Milton wishes here to associate himself only indirectly with what he seems to regard as the legendary background of this belief—as distinct from the "basic truth" that he, the poet, is enunciating.

marks the end of his career. For Satan has been judged by the
Son, it is true, but is still to be judged—has been punished,
but is yet to be punished—when, as the Father tells the Son,

> at one sling
> Of thy victorious Arm, well-pleasing Son,
> Both *Sin*, and *Death*, and yawning *Grave* at last
> Through Chaos hurl'd, obstruct the mouth of Hell
> For ever, and seal up his ravenous Jaws.
> Then Heav'n and Earth renew'd shall be made pure
> To sanctify that shall receive no stain.
>
> (X. 633–39)

F. T. Prince demonstrates a sense of this biblical paradox
when he suggests that

> *Paradise Lost* is prophetic as well as 'historical'; it takes us
> from eternity to eternity, from the eternity before the uni-
> verse was created to the eternity after it will be dissolved.
> The story which began with the revolt of the angels will end
> only with the Last Judgement, the end of the world as we
> know it.[25]

Meanwhile, the struggle (with Satan and his demons at the
center of the assault), however symbolic, goes on.

In the scene, for instance, of the Judgment by the Son in
Book X (ll. 163–209), Milton not only painstakingly identifies
Satan with the Serpent (ll. 171–74), but details for us as well
the future fulfillment of "this Oracle" (X. 182), in terms that
clearly anticipate Michael's explanation to Adam (in Book XII)
of the said conflict between Satan and the incarnate Son of
God (ll. 384–95). As Michael puts it,

---

25. "On the Last Two Books of *Paradise Lost*," *Milton's Epic Poetry*, ed. C. A.
Patrides, p. 235.

> Which hee, who comes thy Saviour, shall recure,
> Not by destroying *Satan*, but his works
> In thee and in thy seed,
>
> (XII. 393–95)

an obvious echo of the words of the narrative voice in X, 190:

> Whom he shall tread at last under our feet.

Nor ought we to forget the poet's comment in Book II, in connection with the "firm Concord" (l. 497) of the devils:

> As if (which might induce us to accord)
> Man hath not hellish foes anow besides.
> That day and night for his destruction wait.
>
> (ll. 503–5)

Satan's metamorphosis in Book X is admittedly allegorical, and thus also symbolic. However, his Heaven-permitted return to his previous form, no less than his involuntary partial loss of his former brightness when we first see him in Book I, is a paradoxical illustration of both his doom and his freedom, both his ultimate control by the Creator and his self-assertive pursuit of Evil, both his potential for degeneration and his will to obduracy. Thus, Satan's punishment by his metamorphosis "in the shape he sinn'd, / According to his doom" (X. 516–17) is neither his final punishment nor the end of his spiteful career. For one thing, however impressive, this event is not the end of *Paradise Lost*. And the poem does not so end because its metaphorical structure (informed from beginning to end by the poet's symbolic vision of the person and function of the Son as the justice of God) extends beyond both the time-scheme and the action of the epic to that distant day when "Hell, her numbers full, / Thenceforth shall be for ever shut" (III. 332–33) and "God shall be All in All" (III. 341).

But for the metamorphosed (and perverted) Satan,

Till then the Curse pronounc't . . . precedes.

(X. 640)

5

Justice and Damnation
in *Paradise Lost*

i

We have so frequently been taught to see the Father's major role in *Paradise Lost* as primarily concerned with justice, and that of the Son as essentially related to mercy, that we have become generally unmindful of the untenable dichotomy within the Godhead of *Paradise Lost*, that such a view unwittingly endorses.[1] After the innumerable discussions about

1. Thomas Kranidas's and J. M. Evans's discussions of Milton's God are good cases in point (see Kranidas, *The Fierce Equation: A Study of Milton's Decorum* [The Hague, 1965], pp. 130–37, and Evans, *Paradise Lost and the Genesis Tradition* [London: Oxford University Press, 1968], pp. 231–41). Despite generally perceptive analyses of Milton's treatment of God in *Paradise Lost*, both Kranidas and Evans leave us with the impression that their basic understanding of Milton's God does not escape what R. M. Frye has called "a vulgar opposition between the love of the Son and the wrath of the Father" (see Roland Mushat Frye, *God, Man, and Satan* [Princeton, N.J.: Princeton University Press, 1960], p. 71). Kranidas correctly observes that justice and mercy are treated decorously and dramatically "in a context of amazing complexities." However, he then makes the altogether too simple distinction between the Father and the Son when he suggests that "God the Father is just, God the Son is loving." This is the same unfortunate dichotomy that underlies the arguments of Malcolm Ross, A. J. A. Waldock, John Peter, and William Empson, with all of whom Kranidas disagrees (see Kranidas, pp. 132–37 and p. 157).

Milton's God (on both sides of the continuing debate), a sense
of the precariousness of such a perspective should at least have
begun to emerge. Yet, a related and more formidable inaccuracy persists in the view that although the Son functions, from
time to time in Milton's poem, as the instrument of the
Father's justice, His essential role in the poem is that of a
mediator and merciful intercessor, as the scene of the Council
in Heaven in Book III, for example, appears to indicate.[2]

Although such a view is partly true, it is, I submit, also
inadequate. For not only is there no genuine distinction in
Paradise Lost between the "Father's justice" and the "Son's
mercy," but there is fundamentally no validity to the conclusion that justice belongs to the Father and mercy to the Son.
In *Paradise Lost*, both what is generally regarded as God's justice and also what is usually thought to be His mercy belong
both to the Father and to the Son. Moreover, what is generally
regarded as God's justice (that is, His anger, His wrath, and
His punishment of evil) is as much a part of the person and
function of the Son as is God's mercy or love. For, in the last
analysis, the Son of God in *Paradise Lost* is the justice (or
righteousness) of God, and that justice is as relevant to good as

---

However, I agree with Kranidas that Waldock, Peter, and Empson insist on a
decorum personae for God that is far too rigid and limited, and that to utilize such a
decorum in the reading of the poem "is an act of critical irresponsibility" (Kranidas, p.
136). It is such rigidity and limitation, with its critically narrow view of Milton's God,
that is able to see the wrath of the God of *Paradise Lost* as "an infirmity he has
forbidden to Man" in the list of the Seven Deadly Sins (John Peter, *A Critique of
Paradise Lost* [Hamden, Conn.: Archon Books, 1970], p. 13), or to interpret "the
picture of God in the poem" as "astonishingly like Uncle Joe Stalin" (William Empson, *Milton's God* [London: Chatto & Windus, 1961], p. 146).

Although Evans seems unwilling to agree that "the whole scene [between the
Father and the Son in Book III] seems calculated to present God in the worst possible
light" (p. 231), his subsequent argument, including even the concessions he is willing
to make to Milton's poetic competence (see pp. 237–41), unwittingly reinforces the
argument that God is presented "in the worst possible light" in the scene in question
in Book III.

2. The formidableness of this inaccuracy lies in its subtle implication that there is,
after all, a fundamental distinction in the poem between *justice*, which belongs essentially to the Father, and *mercy*, which belongs essentially to the Son.

it is to evil, as pertinent to creative and restorative growth as it is to destructive inertia and apostasy, and as applicable to the creature's ultimate salvation as it is to his decisive damnation.

An important example of all of this occurs during the War in Heaven in *Paradise Lost* when the Son goes out to quell the rebellious foes. In the Father's address to the Son, before the latter departs to punish the rebels, the Father assigns to the Son the most remarkable titles, at the same time leaving no doubt either about the Son's relationship to the Father or about the Son's significance as the very *expression* of the Godhead:

> Effulgence of my Glory, Son belov'd,
> Son in whose face invisible is beheld
> Visibly, what by Deity I am,
> And in whose hand what by Decree I do,
> Second Omnipotence. . . .
>
> (VI. 680–84)

This is exactly the impression that the poet encourages, at the end of the Father's speech, when he tells us:

> He said, and on his Son with Rays direct
> Shone full; hee all his Father full exprest
> Ineffably into his face receiv'd,
> And thus the filial Godhead answering spake.
>
> (VI. 719–22)

The Son's reply is equally remarkable. For not only does He confirm everything the Father and the narrative voice have just declared, but he also insists on a capability that must surely shock the inattentive reader accustomed to thinking of the Son in terms of mercy and love:

> But whom thou hat'st, I hate, *and can put on*

> *Thy terrors, as I put thy mildness on,*
> Image of thee in all things.
>
> (VI. 734–36)[3]

Not much later, the narrative voice, in turn, confirms the validity of the Son's statement, when we are told:

> So spake the Son, and into terror chang'd
> His count'nance too severe to be beheld
> And full of wrath bent on his Enemies.
>
> (VI. 824–26)

Both the Son's countenance as it is portrayed in these lines and his harsh words about his capacity to hate and terrify His enemies would, with their belligerence and terror, repel the toughest sensibility—except for an important fact too seldom noted and not sufficiently analyzed: the Son's intervening speech to the loyal Host (VI. 801–23).

This significant speech of the Son in *Paradise Lost* is crucial for an accurate understanding not only of the relationship between the Father and the Son and of the person and function of the Son as God's justice, but especially of the whole issue of justice and damnation in *Paradise Lost*. For what the Son asserts, in part, is:

> but of this cursed crew
> The punishment to other hand belongs;
> Vengeance is his, or whose he sole appoints;
> Number to this day's work is not ordain'd
> Nor multitude, stand only and behold
> God's indignation on these Godless pour'd
> By mee; *not you but mee they have despised,*
> *Yet envied; against mee is all thir rage,*
> *Because the Father,* t'whom in Heav'n supreme
> Kingdom and Power and Glory appertains,

---

3. Italics mine.

Hath honor'd me according to his will.
Therefore to mee thir doom he hath assigned.
(VI. 806–17)[4]

Although the Son's entire speech reverberates with several
echoes from both the Old and the New Testaments,[5] one
point, in particular, stands out: the Son, who has been hon-
ored by His glorious and supreme Father, has been both envied by the rebellious angels, and *despised.* In fact, the thrust of
what the Son is saying here (J. H. Adamson's suggestion that
"Milton's War in Heaven is an adaptation of the *Merkabah*
theme" notwithstanding)[6] is that the "doom" of the rebellious
angels has been "assign'd" to Him by the Father precisely
because it is He who has been "envied," "despised," and raged
against by the rebellious angels. At the same time, the Son
clearly indicates that it is "God's indignation" that is being
"pour'd" on the rebellious angels—as He puts it—"By mee."
For "Vengeance is his, *or whose he sole appoints.*" In short, the
Son is both the "sole" *instrument* of "God's indignation" and
His "Vengeance," and the *substantive reason* for that "indignation" and "Vengenance" in the first place—because, as the
Son points out,

> not you but mee they have despised,
> Yet envied; against mee is all thir rage.

In the end, the burden of the whole affair comes to rest on the
rebellious angels' *despite* for the Son, whose action against
them is the direct result (sanctioned by the Father and carried

---

4. Italics mine.
5. Regarding God's Vengeance, see Deut. 32:35, Psalm 94:1, Romans 12:19, and
Heb. 10:30; in regard to despising the Son of God or God Himself, see Isa. 53:3, Luke
10:16, and 1 Thess. 4:8; and concerning the Son's exaltation by the Father, see Phil.
2:9–11.
6. "The War in Heaven: *The Merkabah,*" *Bright Essence: Studies in Milton's Theology,*
ed. W. B. Hunter, C. A. Patrides, and J. H. Adamson (Salt Lake City, Utah:
University of Utah Press, 1971), p. 113.

out by the Son) of their despite—which is, in effect, the ultimate act of rejection, since it is no less than malice, hatred, contempt, and scorn.

In this context, the curious behavior of Satan and his peers, throughout the entire poem, of never even mentioning the Son of God, whose exaltation was the reason for their rebellion in the first place, and who was the direct instrument of their punishment and consignment to Hell, appears to be, in part, the poet's apt representation of the very malice, hatred, contempt, and scorn that the rebellious angels exhibited by their defiance of the Son while they were still in Heaven.[7] From this perspective also, the whole question of Satan's damnation in *Paradise Lost* begins to clarify itself. For not only is the Son the "sole" appointed instrument of "God's indignation" against apostasy, but He is also, in this specific instance, the very object of Satan's defiance and scorn. In this regard also, the Father's exaltation of the Son as His "image" (V. 784) and only-begotten (V. 603–4), explicitly associated with the Father's Decree and command (V. 602–15), takes on the added dimension of the Son's direct identification with the Father's instrumental, creative testing of the loyalty of the angelic Host, reinforcing and confirming the Son's person and function as the fullest expression and the indispensable instrument of God's justice.

But more than that, as the direct object of Satan's defiance and scorn, the Son emerges from this entire episode as the decisive factor, the inescapable point of reference for all response and relationships in the world of *Paradise Lost*. Thus, by contemptuously defying and despising the Son, Satan

---

7. C. A. Patrides' query ("Might we not conclude that the fallen angels' failure to speak of their archenemy argues that, for them at least, the Father and the Son are not differentiated?") is feasible, and reinforces my suggestion that an offense against one member of the Godhead is, in effect, an offense against the entire Godhead. See Patrides, "The Godhead in *Paradise Lost:* Dogma or Drama?" in *Bright Essence*, p. 74. See also section iv of the present chapter.

tramples upon the very source of his fidelity, virtue, worth, and *justice*—that is to say, upon the very sustenance of his integrity. Thus, Satan's defiance and rejection of the Son plunges him into a process of moral disintegration (and alienation—from his own, true nature, as well as from God) that is as decisive and as inevitable as the Father's Decree and command to the angelic Host in Book V were requisite and irrevocable.

ii

The popular and persistent view of a dichotomy in *Paradise Lost* between the "Father's justice" and the "Son's mercy" (with the erroneous implication that God's justice is strictly and exclusively an instrument of His wrath) is not supported by the ample and convincing evidence to the contrary in Milton's poem.[8] But more significantly, in *Paradise Lost* it is not a matter of God's justice merely being linked with His mercy. Rather, as the central fact of the poem's world, the Son actualizes the very righteousness (or justice) of God. Moreover, the Son actualizes God's righteousness or justice entirely in keeping with the Godhead's essentially creative and inducing processes, which operate *in their totality* to enhance God's creation—either by rigorous or lenient, woeful or compatible, circumstances.

It is precisely this expression of God's righteousness or justice (the totality of the divine concern for the creature's continuously creative and restorative growth—based on an equally vigilant and positive response to the divine ways) that we see especially at work in the case of the postlapsarian Adam and Eve. This "totality of the divine concern," which is sim-

---

8. See, for example, III. 139–40, 225, 306–7, 323–33, 384–96; V. 597, 720; VI. 679, 720, 722, 734–35, 801–66; VII. 175; X. 86, 97, 101, 163–91, 633–37; XII. 311–12, 546–47.

ply another way of talking about God's justice as Milton represents it in *Paradise Lost*, is evident, for example, in the poem's poignant close (XII. 641–49).

Adam and Eve obviously regret that they must leave Paradise, "so late thir happy seat" (1. 642); nevertheless, they depart with a renewed and confident faith, for they can now appreciate the virtue of freely fulfilling the divine creative purposes for them and of responding to God's justice with an equally creative sense of responsibility. "Some natural tears they dropp'd" (1. 645), a perfectly normal reaction to the loss of a cherished gift; yet, just as *normally* they "wip'd them soon" (1. 645), for they know that they can once again entrust themselves to God's justice.

Despite their renewed faith and confidence in that justice, however, Adam and Eve must face the new circumstances with which that very justice confronts them. Yet, we can sense, imbedded in these final lines of the poem, the implicit thought that even this inevitable departure from Paradise is not simply a matter of *punishment* for the Fall, but another in a continuing series of trials—tests of their freedom and their responsibility (that is, of their personal dignity) in their relationship with each other, but especially in their relationship with God. When we see them for the last time, they are poignantly human—but also fundamentally at peace. Moreover, we can sense that their future motto will be the essence of Adam's final conversation with Michael—so important for their continuously vigilant response to God's creative and continuously challenging justice (XII. 557–87).

This very sense of God's creative and continuously challenging justice is evident in the instructions that the Father gives to Michael at the beginning of Book XI (11. 104–17), after the Son, interceding for the penitent Adam and Eve, has presented to the Father their prayers. That Adam and Eve, "th' unholy" (1. 106) must leave the "hallow'd ground" (1. 106) of Paradise is irrevocable. However, the Father instructs

Michael to send them out "without remorse" (1. 105) aiid to "dismiss them not disconsolate" (1. 113). Further, not only is Michael instructed to hide all terror from them, but he is also to disclose to Adam the entire future, including God's promise of a new covenant with men. However, because Adam and Eve have sinned (and in spite of their penitence), Michael is instructed to "denounce / To them and to thir Progeny from thence / Perpetual banishment" (11. 106–8). At the same time, he is to "send them forth, though sorrowing, yet in peace" (1. 117). It is especially this dialectical process that exemplifies the unique, paradoxical nature and function of the justice of God in *Paradise Lost*.

Michael proves to be an excellent teacher, compassionately reassuring Adam of God's continuing concern (XI. 349–53). However, lest Adam should, in his relief and joy, become forgetful of the dialectical nature and function of God's justice, Michael is equally careful to remind him of the inescapable responsibility of all creatures to respond, with reason and discipline, to the challenges of the divine justice. For, as Michael puts it,

> so shalt thou lead
> Safest thy life, and best prepar'd endure
> Thy mortal passage when it comes.
>
> (XI. 364–66)

A further significant example of the creative and restorative nature and function of God's justice in *Paradise Lost* occurs in the opening scenes of Book X, where Milton describes the actual judgment of Adam and Eve by the Son. From the Father's commissioning of the Son to judge the fallen pair to the compassionate action of the Son, when He

> disdain'd not to begin
> Thenceforth the form of servant to assume,
> As when he wash'd his servants' feet, so now

> As Father of his Family he clad
> Thir nakedness with Skins of Beasts. . . ,
>   but inward nakedness, much more
> Opprobrious, with his Robe of righteousness,
>   (X. 213–22)

the whole representation is a graphic illustration of the paradoxical nature and dialectical function of God's justice. In the action of the Son, God's justice characteristically reaches out both to destroy the demonic forces of evil (X. 182–91) that had entrenched themselves in man and also to renovate man's consequently impaired faculties of reason and will in preparation for a gradual and progressive restoration.[9] Not only is the Son aware, for instance, of the sacrifice necessary to effect man's redemption (X. 71–77), but Adam becomes progressively aware (by an excruciating process of self-justification, then confusion, then despair, then remorse and penitence) of his desperate need for restoration.

At the end of Adam's soliloquy, for instance, not only does he admit that the responsibility for his Fall was solely his (and Eve's [X. 836–37]), not God's (X. 832–33), but he expresses the wish that, just as "all the blame lights due" (X. 833) on him for his own corruption, "so might the wrath" (X. 834). Adam can express such a wish only because he has been judged earlier *by the Son*, who did so judge him that he has come to realize, as he admits, "in mee all / Posterity stands curst" (X. 817–18).

In one of his most dramatically powerful portrayals in *Paradise Lost*, Milton represents (through Adam's painful experiences) the sobering nature of God's justice in the face of apostasy and the perversion of the creative processes of the

---

9. Milton's understanding of man's renovation and regeneration, in terms of their origin, process, and essential purpose, is clearly stated in *De Doctrina Christiana* (Book I, chapter 18). Cf. *Paradise Lost*, III. 173–97.

poem's world. Not only does Adam cry out painfully to his Conscience (X. 842–44), but he literally writhes upon the ground in despair, cursing his very creation; accusing Death and Truth and Divine Justice itself of "tardy execution" (X. 852); and shamelessly abusing Eve, belligerently spurning her effort to console him with her soft words (X. 850–908). Eve, for her part, is no less distraught, as her physical appearance and her pitiful remarks make clear (X. 910–36).

What Adam says about "Justice Divine" is of particular interest for our discussion. For, fallen as he is, by his willful perversion of his natural faculties, Adam completely loses his prelapsarian perspective, even accusing divine justice of not being just, *for being kind*, and executing judgment in a way that Adam, now blind to the truth regarding his relationship with God, fails to understand:

> Shall Truth fail to keep her word,
> Justice Divine not hast'n to be just?
> But Death comes not at call, Justice Divine
> Mends not her slowest pace for prayers or cries.
> (X. 856–59)

Little does Adam realize that his own earlier reasoning held both the clue to his present query and the essence of the meaning of God's *justice* in *His* relationship to men. For in answer to his own confusion regarding what to him was the "inexplicability of God's justice" (X. 754–55), Adam notes that his punishment, in the final analysis, is just because he can have nothing to do with the decision—as to *when*, we might add, to punish, or *how* to punish, or even *if* to punish, since that decision is entirely, as Adam correctly notes, "at his Will" (X. 768)—that is to say, at God's will.

It is especially in his portrayal of the Council in Heaven in Book III that Milton characterizes the practical application and effect of God's justice—in his delineation of the developing stages of the Son's exemplary response to the Father's inducing ways. It is neither possible nor necessary to deny the contention that the Father "seems to be playing to the gallery of his auditors, the Son and the unfallen angeles,"[10] in this scene. *Impossible*, because that is the effect we get from Milton's presentation of the Father; and *unnecessary*, because that is precisely the effect Milton wishes us to get. However, to go on, as John Peter suggests, to regard the Father's role in this scene as "little better than celestial hypocrisy"[11] is to fail to ask a very basic question about that role: *Why such a role?*—both in terms of what actually happens in the scene and in terms of the Father's ironic (even if anthropomorphic) pose.[12]

Milton explains in the "Argument" to Book III that God clears Himself of all responsibility for man's Fall, *"having created Man free and able enough to have withstood his Tempter: yet declares his purpose of grace towards him."*[13] Exactly the same point is made in the corresponding lines of the poetry that follows (III. 98–99, 116–19, and 130–34). Moreover, what the Son actually does in His first speech, according to the "Argument," is to praise the Father for His promise of grace toward man. As Milton puts it, *"the Son of God renders praises to his Father for the manifestation of his gracious purpose towards Man."* The poetic parallel is no less interesting:

> O Father, gracious was that word which clos'd
> Thy sovran sentence, that Man should find grace.
> (III. 144–45)

Obviously, the Son would hardly have used such words at the

10. Peter, p. 12.
11. *Ibid.*
12. Cf. Barker, "The Relevance of Regeneration," p. 69. See also Michael Wilding, *Milton's Paradise Lost* (Sydney: Sydney University Press, 1969), pp. 64–65.
13. Hughes, *John Milton: Complete Poems and Major Prose*, p. 257.

very beginning of His first speech unless the Father had in fact so manifested His gracious purpose toward man.

Milton confirms this fact toward the end of the scene, for it is as "Father of Mercy and Grace" (III. 401) that the angels hail *the Father*. Moreover, what the angels go on to sing of the Father, as well as the manner in which this is expressed by the poet, is most significant:

> Father of Mercy and Grace, thou didst not doom
> So strictly, but much more to pity incline:
> No sooner did thy dear and only Son
> Perceive thee purpos'd not to doom frail Man
> So strictly, but much more to pity inclin'd. . . .
>
> (III. 401–5)

We should note here not only the use of the past tense, but also the obvious emphatic repetition of the thought: *not to doom so strictly, but much more to pity inclined*. Moreover, however promptly the Son responded to the Father's inclination to be merciful, He did, after all, *respond*. Clearly, the angels have absolutely no doubt either about the appropriateness of the title they are ascribing to the Father, or about the initial indication by the Father to be merciful, and the consequent response by the Son to the Father's declared intention.

At the same time, neither the true nature of Milton's *God* nor the fact that it is He who initiates the whole process of the Atonement should encourage us to lose sight of the unstated purpose or of the dramatic significance of the scene. The fact is that the burden of the scene of the Council in Heaven rests on the Son's exemplary response to the Father's inducing ways, and everything else in the scene is intended to contribute to this important effect.[14]

---

14. See Barker, "The Relevance of Regeneration," p. 68. Cf. Stella P. Revard, "The Dramatic Function of the Son in *Paradise Lost:* A Commentary on Milton's 'Trinitarianism,' " *JEGP* 66 (1967): 45–58. Revard's understanding of the Son's exer-

It is only from this perspective, for instance, that that section of Book III which deals with the crux of Milton's meaning (11. 210–16)—and which has evidently caused some readers the greatest difficulty[15]—becomes intelligible as a vital part of the Father's conscious effort to challenge the Son and to induce from Him a response that is both creative and exemplary. Isabel MacCaffrey's point is well taken that the great question with which the Father's second speech concludes "leads from theory to practice, from the 'great idea' to history."[16] This, in fact, is the point of the entire episode. Far from being a theological blunder, the great question that the Father poses (III. 213–16) is entirely consistent with His essential purpose of inducing from the Son a loving and sacrificial response. No less consistent with the Father's purpose is the rigid satisfaction of His justice. For, by associating the great question with the rigid demand that His justice be satisfied, the Father is able to demonstrate, through the exemplary and creative response of the Son, both the essentially positive and practically inducing nature and function of His justice and the crucial significance for all His creatures of the Son as the fullest and most effective expression of that justice. Thus, both the Father's apparently unreasonable demand and His seemingly incredible question are, in terms of His consciously adopted role, just as logical and necessary an instrument of His larger creative and restorative purposes for the Son as His justice, expressed and implemented in this very scene and elsewhere in the poem (e.g., Books X, XI, and XII), serves as a similar instrument to induce from all His creatures a positive and creative emulation of the Son's response.

---

cise of His free will is especially instructive and reinforces her thesis that "the Son's career in *Paradise Lost* is a progress from good to better; he is constantly in the process of proving himself by assuming and exercising more power" (p. 50).

15. See, for example, Peter, pp. 13–14, and C. A. Patrides, *Milton and the Christian Tradition* (London: Oxford University Press, 1966), p. 158.

16. Isabel G. MacCaffrey, "The Theme of *Paradise Lost*, Book III," *New Essays on Paradise Lost*, ed. Thomas Kranidas, p. 74.

iii

[Totally different from the creative and exemplary response
of the Son is that of Satan's complete commitment to evil,
reinforced by a firm and fierce incorrigibility. Consequently,
Satan finds himself enmeshed in a progressively tightening
web of lies, distortions, perversities, and an all-consuming
egotism. Yet, all of this would say very little if, in fact, Satan
were not responsible for his condition, as has occasionally
been suggested.[17] And from a purely abstract and essentially
metaphysical perspective, one can, of course, maintain such a
point of view indefinitely.]However, though rather trite and
somewhat prosaic to say so, *Paradise Lost* is not a treatise on
metaphysics, nor even on theology (as neither, incidentally, is
the Bible), and in the poem's world, the responsibility for
Satan's perverse condition lies where it rightly belongs: with
Satan himself.

For example, not only does the Father, contemplating the
perversity of the fallen angels, declare in Book III;

> The first sort by thir own suggestion fell,
> Self-tempted, self-depraved; Man falls deceiv'd
> By the other first: Man therefore shall find grace,
> The other none,
>
> (III. 129–32)

but the poet makes abundantly clear, at several places
throughout the epic,[18] the unavoidable consequences of

---

17. See, e.g., Empson, pp. 69–70.
18. For example, in the words of

(i) the poet: I. 44–48, 53–54, 70–72, 209–20, 607–8; IV. 15–23, 846–50; IX.
    467–70; and X. 509–17;
(ii) the Father: III. 84–86 and V. 611–15;
(iii) the Son: VI. 736–39;
(iv) the unfallen angels: IV. 570–71, 823–24, 835–40; V. 541–43, 883–85; VI.
    172–73, and 181;
(v) the fallen angels: I. 141–42; II. 85–89, 158–59, 197–99, 315–31, and 377–78;
(vi) Satan himself: II. 29–30; IV. 73–78, 86–92, 375, 508–11, and 889–90;
(vii) even Death: II. 693–97 and 699–700.

angelic apostasy, especially because, as the Father tells the Son during His first speech in Book III,

> Such I created all th' Ethereal Powers
> And Spirits, both them who stood and them who fail'd;
> Freely they stood who stood, and fell who fell;
> (III. 100–102)

and not much later, in the same speech:

> I form'd them free, and free they must remain,
> Till they enthrall themselves; I else must change
> Thir nature, and revoke the high Decree
> Unchangeable, Eternal, which ordain'd
> Thir freedom: they themselves ordain'd thir fall.
> (III. 124–28)

This is exactly Satan's point during his soliloquy on Mount Niphates:

> but other Powers as great
> Fell not, but stand unshak'n, from within
> Or from without, to all temptations arm'd.
> Hadst thou the same free Will and Power to stand?
> Thou hadst.
> (IV. 63–67)

He does try to excuse himself, nevertheless, by way of an abortive rationalization (IV. 67–70), but he is forced, by his own reasoning, to admit that

> against his thy will
> Chose freely what it now so justly rues.
> (IV. 71–72)

Satan is right, moreover, about "what it now so justly rues," as he painfully, but accurately, makes clear (IV. 73–102).

Yet, this is not the largest of Satan's problems. Much more

damning is Satan's irrevocable commitment to evil, and his persistent abuse not only of himself but also of others. Satan is quite right when he declares on Niphates' top:

> all Good to me is lost,
>
> (IV. 109)

for he has just dismissed yet another chance for his restoration[19] with his perverse "Farewell Remorse" (IV. 109). But more important is the selfish way in which he abuses others. Quite apart from his tyrannical control over his infernal followers, Satan abuses the personal freedom and dignity of everyone whom he encounters, including even the two other members of the infernal trinity. The epitome of his abuse of others is reached in his temptation of Eve, illustrated most forcefully by the poet in another of Satan's soliloquies— this time in Book IX, as he prepares to implement his evil strategy against Man:

> all good to me becomes
> Bane, and in Heav'n much worse would be my state.
> But neither here seek I, no nor in Heav'n
> To dwell, unless by Maistring Heav'n's Supreme;
> Nor hope to be myself less miserable
> By what I seek, *but others to make such*
> *As I, though thereby worse to me redound.*
>
> (IX. 122–28)[20]

---

19. Profoundly concerned with demonstrating the reasonableness of retributive justice, both St. Aquinas and St. Augustine, for example, erroneously insist on the incapacity of the evil angelic will to change once it has become evil. Simply put, men may choose to repent; sinful angels may not, because they *can not* (see Aquinas, *Summa Theologica*, LXIV. 2, and Augustine, *The City of God*, XII. 9, as well as XI. 13, where Augustine evinces considerable confusion about this matter).

In *Paradise Lost*, Raphael's explanation to Adam about angelic freedom is radically different (see V. 535–40). It is only on this basis that the integrity of the divine justice can be maintained, in regard to evil angels. For what emerges is the plain fact that both the responsibility for, and the actualization of, the creature's choice—in his response to the Creator—is entirely his own doing.
20. Italics mine.

Notwithstanding his attempt to justify his motives by talking about revenge, Satan has—despite his superficially heroic stance and tone here—descended to quite base things. Once again, he is right when he soliloquizes:

> But what will not Ambition and Revenge
> Descend to? who aspires must down as low
> As high he soar'd, obnoxious first or last
> To basest things.
>
> (IX. 168–71)

In the end, Satan reveals the depth of his degeneration and the extent of his malice when, most significantly, not only does he declare his intention to pursue to the very end his career of spitefulness, but he does so in language that is pointedly reminiscent of the beginning of his spiteful career:

> on him who next
> Provokes my envy, *this new Favorite*
> *Of Heav'n*, this Man of Clay, *Son of despite*.
>
> (IX. 174–76)

One can hardly miss the implied association between Satan's envy and contemptuous definance of the Son (VI. 812–13), which started the War in Heaven, and his present allusion to Man both as the "new Favorite / Of Heav'n" and as the "Son of despite." The similarity is also strengthened by Satan's recollection of his motive for his rebellion in Heaven, as indicated by his admission that he aspired "to the highth of Deity" (IX. 167). By comparison, Satan confirms his own sense of the enormity of his intended evil against Man, since his rebellion against the Son earned the dire consequences (because of its enormity) that he now partly laments (IX. 163–72). Evidently, Satan expects the worst possible results for his contemplated evil against Man, as his words "Let it, I

reck not" (IX. 173) attest, as does his recognition of the sui-
cidal nature of revenge:

> Revenge, at first though sweet,
> Bitter ere long back on itself recoils.
>
> (IX. 171–72)

⌈ Moreover, Satan's association of ambition with revenge, the
self-destructive nature of which he admits, not only corrobo-
rates his admission in the preceding line that he aspired "to
the highth of Deity," but defines his present ambition in the
baser terms of contemplated and malicious revenge against
innocent Man, whom now he even slanders in terms appropriate to the state of his own degeneration as compared with his
words of some regret and sympathy in IV. 358–92.⌋In practical terms, Satan's abuse of others is the best evidence in
Paradise Lost for both his degeneration and his perversion of the
creative and restorative processes of the poem's world. Merritt
Hughes is right that in the world of *Paradise Lost*, Satan is "the
archetypal tyrant."[21] Hughes also correctly associates Satan
with "the society which Michael describes to Adam as doomed
to servitude 'When upstart Passions catch the Government /
From Reason' [XII. 88–89]."[22]

As significant as the general applicability to Satan of the
passage at the beginning of Book XII are specific sections of
the passage that elucidate not only the general perversity of
tyranny and the loss of rational liberty, but also particular
characteristics of the tyrant's career. A number of these
characteristics aptly apply to Satan. For example, ll. 36–39
in Michael's description of Nimrod, whom Milton, unlike
Gen. 11:1–9, directly associates with the story of the confusion of tongues during the construction of the Tower of Babel.

21. *Ten Perspectives on Milton*, p. 166.
22. *Ibid.*, p. 195.

With Satan's specific reference to "ambition and revenge" in IX. 168 (just briefly examined), and with echoes of Satan's rebellion in Books V and VI scattered throughout his soliloquy in Book IX, these lines in Book XII read like a commentary on important aspects of Satan's career in *Paradise Lost:*

> And from Rebellion shall derive his name,
> Though of Rebellion others he accuse.
> Hee with a crew, whom like Ambition joins
> With him or under him to tyrannize.

Not only is the last line of the passage interestingly vague (with its use of "with him or under him"), with the implication of the tyrant exercising his tyranny even over his peers, but 1. 36 recalls the meaning of "Satan," which is "enemy" or "adversary"; 1. 37 is reminiscent of Satan's charge of tyranny against God (see I. 124 and X. 466); and 1. 38, if applied to Satan, speaks for itself. Consequently, it is not at all difficult, by the time one gets to the *locus classicus* in *Paradise Lost* of Milton's discussion of the loss of "Rational Liberty" (XII. 82) and the resulting tyranny (in XII. 79–101) to make a direct association between Satan and "the archetypal tyrant."

Equally applicable to Satan's tyrannical career in *Paradise Lost* is the second half of the passage, in which Michael explains to Adam the inevitable consequences for nations that abuse their "Rational Liberty." Of particular significance is the instrument that deprives such nations of their outward freedom. As Michael puts it,

> sometimes Nations will decline so low
> From virtue, which is reason, *that no wrong,*
> *But Justice, and some fatal curse annext*
> Deprives them of thir outward liberty,
> Thir inward lost.
>
> (XII. 97–101)[23]

---

23. Italics mine.

That "Justice" and "some fatal curse" are so explicitly associated here as the instrument of deprivation of "thir outward
liberty" is, in itself, most important. For the unavoidable conclusion is that, in the case of "Nations" that abuse their inward
liberty to the point of its disappearance from among them,
"Justice," annexing "some fatal curse," expresses itself against
them in a manner that completes their loss of liberty by de-
priving them of their outward freedom. It is significant, however, not only that "Justice" employs, as it were, a fatal *curse* to
effect its objective, but also that such a process is "no wrong."
That is to say, the "fatal curse," which under ordinary circumstances would be considered a grave misfortune if not a
gross *injustice,* becomes—in the face of such a repudiation or
contemptuous disregard of virtue—an inevitable and just
agency for the punishment of such dissolute living.

Moreover, Michael is quite careful not to create the impression that this "Justice," which annexes "some fatal curse," is
fate or chance or undeserved misfortune of some sort. Rather,
he sets up an almost exact comparison between nations and
individuals (at least by implication), and in the case of individuals, says Michael:

> Therefore since hee permits
> Within himself unworthy Powers to reign
> Over free Reason, *God in Judgment just*
> Subjects him from without to violent Lords;
> Who oft as undeservedly enthrall
> His outward freedom.
>
> (XII. 90–95)

Clearly, the "fatal curse" annexed by "Justice" is as *just* as it is
inescapable because it performs, along with "Justice," exactly
the same function—in the case of nations—as "God in Judgment just" performs in the case of individuals: subjecting them
to a loss of outward freedom. In short, the "fatal curse" annexed by "Justice" is an important part of God's "Judgment
just."

It is precisely this principle of annexing evil forces for the
punishment of evil that applies to Satan, the "author of evil"
(VI. 262). For nowhere in the poem does Milton tell us that
God's justice vindictively seeks to torment even those who are
obdurately evil. Rather, what we learn about the world of
Paradise Lost in connection with the processes of judgment
upon apostasy is, as Michael tells us,

> God in Judgment just
> Subjects him from without to violent Lords;
>
> (XII. 92–93)

and as he further explains,

> Justice, and some fatal curse annext
> Deprives them of thir outward liberty,
> Thir inward lost.
>
> (XII. 99–101)

For it is not God's justice that tyrannizes over either the evil or
the good. Rather, regarding evil in *Paradise Lost*, the cause, as
well as the result, begins with the wicked and remains (with
the inescapable and decisive endorsement of God's justice)
upon the wicked. Significantly, in the single instance in
Paradise Lost where the word *damnation* is actually used, this is
exactly the point that is being made by the narrative voice, in
connection with Satan's malicious tyranny over others:

> That with reiterated crimes he might
> Heap on himself damnation, while he sought
> Evil to others.
>
> (I. 214–16)

Understandably disturbed by "the great losses" to the
human race outlined by Michael in Books XI and XII, W. J.
Grace suggests that it would appear that "any experiment in

freedom entails big losses," and that "God must then have thought that freedom was worth such a price."[24] Apart from the fact that in the world of the poem, God's creating all His creatures with "Rational Liberty" (XII. 82) is no "experiment" or gamble, as the poet is careful to point out throughout the epic,[25] the answer to Grace's query is unequivocally affirmative. However, two observations are of crucial importance here. First, the reader, it would appear, is not intended by the poet to accept such losses "calmly," as Grace appears to understand. On the contrary, he ought indeed to react with an abhorrence comparable to that of Adam, but also with a two-fold recognition of the reprehensible nature of evil and of the possibility of still exercising one's rational liberty for good in a situation in which, most realistically,

> so shall the World go on,
> To good malignant, to bad men benign,
> Under her own weight groaning.
>
> (XII. 537–39)

Second, the poet appears indeed to be suggesting that it is only such a recognition on the part of the reader (as is finally true for Adam in the imaginative experience of the poem) that will correctly define the heinousness of evil and injustice and, simultaneously, the desirability of good and true liberty in the relationships that all men are required to establish and vigilantly to pursue.

Nor can we justifiably read into the total pattern of the poem the mistaken notion, so frequently attributed to Milton, that the exercise of such rational liberty requires an existential situation in which evil is as necessary as good and injustice as

---

24. William J. Grace, *Ideas in Milton* (Notre Dame, Ind.: University of Notre Dame Press, 1968), p. 99.
25. See, for example, III. 100–116; IV. 66–67; V. 233–37, 529–40; and IX. 1173–74.

indispensable as liberty for right human choice. Milton, Irene
Samuel reminds us,

> did not hold that virtue needs evil—the doctrine sometimes
> misread into *Areopagitica*—and he did not condone the evils
> of willed injustice. Satan is the fit target of just anger in
> *Paradise Lost* as in himself and his policies he sums up every
> evil detail in the human panorama of Books XI and XII.[26]

Satan is the "fit target" of damnation in *Paradise Lost* because,
as he so accurately confesses:

> never can true reconcilement grow
> Where wounds of deadly hate have pierc'd so deep,
> (IV. 98–99)

especially when such "deadly hate" actualizes itself in a perverse and tyrannical abuse of others.

As Death so appropriately asserts in Book II, Satan is—we,
too, realize—"Hell-doom'd" (1. 697). For unlike Adam, who
makes a positive and re-creative about-face (X. 1097–1104),
Satan never does.

iv

The central argument of this entire study would suddenly
collapse if it turns out to be true that in *Paradise Lost* God's
justice has very little to do with His righteousness as Milton
understood the latter; that both God's justice and His righteousness have little or nothing, in turn, to do with the person
and function of the Son in *Paradise Lost;* and that all three of
these aspects of Milton's representations in the poem (God's
justice, His righteousness, and the Son) are not particularly

---

26. Irene Samuel, *Dante and Milton: The Commedia and Paradise Lost* (Ithaca, N.Y.:
Cornell University Press, 1966), p. 182.

related to the creative and restorative processes inherent in the poem's world and possibly reinforced by these three supposedly interrelated aspects of *Paradise Lost*.

Moreover, the fact that Milton might have been a competent student of the Scriptures; or that he might have accepted the essentially biblical view of God's justice as identical with His righteousness and as restorative and re-creative rather than as primarily concerned with rewards and punishments; or that his view of the Son of God might have been in distinct accord with the basic Christological emphasis in the New Testament; or that he transferred these characteristics of biblical theology, filtered through his poetic sensibility, to the work that is now *Paradise Lost*—will each (and all together) mean nothing for a discussion of this sort, unless it were true that these various assumptions could be illustrated as factually viable in terms of what we actually find in *Paradise Lost*.

The answer to the first set of suggestions is that *they do*—that is, they have everything to do with one another regarding Milton's understanding of God's justice as it is illustrated in *Paradise Lost*. And the answer to the second set of probabilities (or improbabilities, as the case might be) is that we ought simply to get about the business, here and now, of trying to determine whether any or all of these suppositions are demonstrable on the basis of the text of *Paradise Lost*. I submit that they are.

The basic issue involved here, and that which goes to the heart of the two general queries above, with their specific propositions, is, first, the extent to which the poet of *Paradise Lost* understood there to be at least a distinct and positive relationship, if not a complete identification, between the two concepts of God's justice and His righteousness in the poem. And second, assuming that he did understand such a relationship to exist, whether he then saw the two terms as distinctly and positively related, in turn, to the Son in *Paradise Lost*. To repeat, my argument is that he did—in both instances.

Although the recent Ingram-Swaim *Concordance to Milton's English Poetry* lists the word *just* (and its derivative forms: *justice, justification, justify,* and *justly*) as being used in *Paradise Lost* eighty-two times,[27] we might more practically approach the question of the possible identification in *Paradise Lost* between *justice* and *righteousness* by examining the relatively fewer instances in the poem of the use of *righteous* (and its derivative form, *righteousness*), which the Ingram-Swaim *Concordance* lists as being used a total of twelve times. It need hardly be said that even in their English forms, the words *justice* and *righteousness* are essentially synonymous[28]—as any good English dictionary will indicate. Three important examples of the use of *righteous* and/or *righteousness* in *Paradise Lost* will have to suffice.

The first of the three selected occurrences of *righteous* in *Paradise Lost* concerns the Son's important speech to the loyal angels during the War in Heaven (specifically, in VI. 801–23), in which the Son, in commending the loyal angels, declares:

> Ye Angels arm'd, this day from Battle rest;
> Faithful hath been your Warfare, and of God
> Accepted, fearless in his *righteous* Cause.
> (VI. 802–4)[29]

As was pointed out earlier in this chapter,[30] the Son's speech to the loyal angels is especially important because it illustrates

---

27. *A Concordance to Milton's English Poetry*, ed. William Ingram and Kathleen Swaim (London: Oxford University Press, 1972), pp. 302–3, 458–59. The following is a breakdown into specific forms of *just* and of *righteous* from the general Ingram-Swaim listing:

Just	*Justice*	*Justification*	*Justify*	*Justly*
52	17	1	2	10

Righteous				*Righteousness*
6				6

28. In the New Testament, the Greek word δίκαιος is translated both as "just" and as "righteous." Cf. chapter 4, n3 above.
29. Italics mine.
30. See section i of the present chapter.

His decisive and inescapable significance in the world of
Paradise Lost, and also because, as the "sole" appointed instrument of "God's indignation" against the rebellious angels who
both envied and despised the Son, the Son confirms Himself
as the indispensable and best expression of God's justice.
Thus, the "righteous Cause" to which the Son refers is the
same "Cause" for which the loyal angels went out against the
rebellious angels in the first place, and on behalf of which the
Son now appears.

Two factors are especially important here. First, the "War-
fare" of the loyal angels, the "punishment" and "Vengeance"
and "doom" to be carried out by the Son against the rebellious
Host, and "God's indignation," which are all for the same
cause, are referred to as God's "righteous Cause." Second,
God's cause, in this instance, is no less than the decisive and
inescapable significance of the Son in the poem's universe (11.
812–16). Thus, God's "righteous Cause" turns out to be both
the function of the Son as God's "sole," appointed instrument
for the punishment of the rebellious angels *and* God's concern
for the Son's decisive and inescapable place in the poem's
world. However, the Son's function as God's "sole," appointed instrument for the punishment of the rebellious angels
is for God's "righteous Cause"—which is the "righteous
Cause" of His Son. Or is it the "Cause" of His "righteous"
Son? The two remaining examples should help us to clarify
the point.

Michael's description to Adam in Book XI (11. 804–21) of
Noah's devotion to God adds another dimension to this discussion. For, as Michael explains,

> One Man except, the only Son of light
> In a dark Age, against example good,
> Against allurement, custom, and a World
> Offended; fearless of reproach and scorn,
> Or violence, hee of thir wicked ways

> Shall them admonish, and before them set
> *The paths of righteousness, how much more safe,*
> *And full of peace,* denouncing wrath to come
> On thir impenitence; and shall return
> Of them derided, but of God observ'd
> *The one just Man alive.*[31]

One fact is indisputable here: Michael refers to Noah as the "one just Man alive," whom—Adam is told—God observed. However, Michael also refers to Noah as "the only Son of light," which, in part, prepares us for Michael's explanation that Noah

> before them set
> The paths of righteousness, how much more safe,
> And full of peace.

For we can readily associate safety and peace with light, and all three qualities with the "paths of righteousness."[32] Yet, Noah's sense of righteousness is not to be exclusively concerned with safety, peace, and light. For, as Michael explains to Adam, Noah will admonish the "degenerate" and "deprav'd" (1. 806) about their wicked ways, and denounce "wrath to come / On thir impenitence." Further, he will not be troubled by reproach and scorn, or be afraid of violence.

In fact, Michael is describing to Adam a truly *just* man—devout and yet courageous, concerned with the gentler qualities of peace, safety, and light, but also with the vigor and prophetic toughness that must accompany admonitions and denouncements. And though he will be derided by the obdurate, his righteousness will be seen and approved by God. As a matter of fact, as Michael continues to reveal to Adam the

---

31. Italics mine.
32. Cf. Proverbs 4:18: "But the path of the just is as a shining light, that shineth more and more unto the perfect day."

story of Noah, it becomes clear that he and his household will be saved "from amidst / A World devote to universal rack." It is because he will be just that Noah will be saved. Equally important is the fact that Michael ascribes to him the epithet *just* because he will set before the wicked the gentler paths of "righteousness." The terms, quite close in usage in *Paradise Lost*, are, in fact, virtually identical here.

The third and final example of Milton's use of *righteous* (here "righteousness") in *Paradise Lost* occurs during Michael's reply to Adam in Book XII concerning the fundamental difference between the Law and the Gospel, the old covenant and the new. It is sufficiently significant to be repeated here, in part:

> that when they see
> Law can discover sin, but not remove,
> Save by those shadowy expiations weak,
> The blood of Bulls and Goats, they may conclude
> Some blood more precious must be paid for Man,
> *Just for unjust, that in such righteousness*
> *To them by Faith imputed, they may find*
> *Justification towards God, and peace*
> *Of Conscience*, which the Law by Ceremonies
> Cannot appease, nor Man the moral part
> Perform, and not performing cannot live.
>   (XII. 289–99)[33]

This important passage in *Paradise Lost* deserves detailed and careful analysis.

Two general observations may be offered. First, it is clear from this passage that Milton not only understood the basic identification of the words *just* and *righteous* (and their several forms), but he also recognized their further identification in theological content and value. Second, the passage cries out for comparison with the equally important discussion (during

---

33. Italics mine.

the scene of the Council in Heaven in Book III) of many of the
same theological points. We ought to observe, for instance,
that XII. 293–97 makes almost the exact theological point as
III. 213–16, and is quite similar, even in regard to the phrases
used (cf. "Just for unjust" in XII. 294 with "just th' unjust to
save" in III. 215).

The immediate point of interest, however, is that in this
third and final example there is indisputable evidence that
Milton was well aware of the theological significance of the
words *just* and *righteous*, as well as of their identification.
Michael's exact words clearly indicate this fact. Michael explains to Adam that because those who will be under the imper-
fection of the Law will come to realize that

> Law can discover sin, but not remove,

they will logically conclude that

> Some blood more precious must be paid for Man,
> Just for unjust . . . .

The repetition here of the phrase *Just for unjust* (in practically
the exact form as it appears in III, 215) indicates both the
similarity and the significance of the two passages in which the
phrase occurs. Moreover, the phrase as it is used here has
exactly the same basic meaning as it does in Book III.[34] Not
only does the juxtaposition of *just* and *unjust* in the present
passage express a distinct contrast between divinity and humanity but, more significantly, it emphasizes the particular
condition, in the "just" and in the "unjust," of *righteousness* —
which occurs in the same line (in XII. 294). Clearly, the condition in the "unjust" is a state of *un*righteousness, since it is

---

34. See chapter 4, section i above.

the "just" who has to pay some "blood more precious" *for* the "unjust."

Thus, in the present passage, the occurrence of the phrase *just for unjust*, in direct association with *righteousness*, leaves no doubt about Milton's understanding of *just* as meaning *righteous* (that is, of "justice"—or "just*ness*," if you will—as meaning "righteous*ness*"). In fact, two clear indications of this understanding of the identification of the two words occur in 11. 294–96.

The first indication of such an understanding by Milton of the identical qualities of *just* and *righteous* occurs in 1. 294, where *righteousness* is modified by *such*, with the whole phrase *such righteousness* referring back to its double antecedent, the payment of "Some blood more precious . . . for Man" (1. 293), and "just" (1. 294). Further, it is the "just" who is the *subject* both of the more precious blood that is paid for Man and of the special righteousness needed by the "unjust." In other words, the "just," who pays the more precious blood for Man, has for Man, the "unjust," the necessary righteousness (or he could not pay the more precious blood). However, the "just" can have such "righteousness" only if he is "righteous"—which is exactly the reason why he is "just."

The second indication of this linguistic and theological identification between *just* and *righteous*—or *justice* and *righteousness*—occurs in 11. 295–97, where *justification*, a form of the word *just*, also occurs. As Michael explains the matter to Adam, the "unjust" (1. 294), who "may find / Justification towards God, and peace / Of Conscience" (11. 295–297), must, in order to find that "justification," have imputed to them "by Faith" (1. 295) the same special "righteousness" that belongs to the "just" who has to pay the "blood more precious . . . for Man." What this means is that unless the "unjust" have "such righteousness" imputed to them "by Faith," they will remain "unjust," and obviously cannot find such justification. Thus, in the final analysis, the justification absolutely depends upon the special righteousness that belongs to the "just." However, the justification can be genuine only if its giver, that is to say, the "just," is also genuine, and the "just," especially regarding justification, can be genuine only if he is "righteous"—which is precisely the reason why he is "just."

The unique characteristics attached to the terms *just* and *righteous* throughout the preceding example must obviously belong to one who is capable of demonstrating their validity and efficacy, thereby confirming the efficacy of his own person and function as the *righteousness* or *justice* of God. In *Paradise Lost*, that individual is the Son of God, whose decisive and overwhelming presence at the center of the poem's world defines the postulates of that world, including His own responsibility to carry out its demanding tasks: first, to quell the Adversary; second, to fulfill the Law; and third, to bring men back to the lost Paradise of peace.

As a matter of fact, this is exactly what *Paradise Lost* is basically all about, as, indeed, it is essentially what the Bible is all about. We would therefore expect that, as aware as he no doubt was about the importance of such a theme, the poet of *Paradise Lost* would leave some indication of his awareness not only of the theological significance of God's justice or righteousness, but especially of his sense of the Son of God as the best expression of that justice. For nothing less than a combination (or identification) of God's justice and the Son's decisive and overwhelming presence can simultaneously quell the Adversary, fulfill the Law, and bring men back to the lost Paradise of peace.

Moreover, we would also expect the poet of *Paradise Lost* to leave an equally unequivocal indication of his awareness not only of the essentially creative and restorative nature of God's justice (that is to say, of the person and function of the Son), but also of the fact that the actualization and expression of that justice cannot be restricted to the rather narrow function of "distribution" and "retribution," as if the Son of God were a mere agent of God's *Law*, with the primary function of rewarding the good and punishing the wicked.

In a brief but profoundly significant passage, immediately following the one just under discussion, Milton leaves us—in less than ten of the most important lines in *Paradise Lost*—an unequivocal indication of his awareness of these salient points. As Michael puts it to Adam,

>   therefore shall not *Moses*, though of God
> Highly belov'd, being but the Minister
> Of Law, his people into *Canaan* lead;
> But Joshua whom the Gentiles *Jesus* call,
> His Name and Office bearing, who shall quell
> The adversary Serpent, and bring back
> Through the world's wilderness long wander'd man
> Safe to eternal Paradise of rest.
>   (XII. 307–14)

This, in the end, is what *Paradise Lost* is saying. And if that should seem too large a claim, then let us concern ourselves essentially with the question of God's justice—looking at the central argument of this study from the perspective of the *new* Joshua, his own "Name and Office bearing," who is by no means "but the Minister of Law."

6

God's Justice and the Poet's Style
in *Paradise Lost*

i

A careful reading of *Paradise Lost* discloses a fundamental paradoxical structure in Milton's major poem, which is less the
result of a kind of poetic Manichaeism ("an unusual bifurcation of the poem," in the words of Christopher Grose, "into
narrative and drama or rhetoric")[1] than the consequence of a
positive circularity, in theme and style, that gives the poem its
coherence and unity. It is precisely such a structure, I submit,
that creates the intense paradoxical tension in the poem, but
that, because of its basic, circular movement, most effectively
unifies the diverse narrative, dramatic, rhetorical, and conven-
tional elements of *Paradise Lost*.

This structural disposition of *Paradise Lost* is, moreover, entirely consistent with Milton's theory of poetry and of the
poet, largely contained in a few limited sections of *An Apology*

---

1. *Milton's Epic Process: Paradise Lost and Its Miltonic Background* (New Haven and
London: Yale University Press, 1973), p. 17.

168

for Smectymnuus, the Preface to Book II of *The Reason of Church Government*, and *Of Education*. In *An Apology for Smectymnuus*, for instance, Milton declares:

> And long it was not after, when I was confirmed in this opinion that he who would not be frustrate of his hope to write well hereafter in laudable things, ought himself to be a true poem, that is, a composition and pattern of the best and honorablest things—not presuming to sing high praises of heroic men or famous cities, unless he have in himself the experience and the practice of all that which is praise-worthy.[2]

Apart from his recognition here of "a true poem" as the common denominator of poetry and of the poet, Milton interestingly insists, even in 1642, on such a "composition and pattern of the best and honorablest things" for poetry and the poet—at a time when he was still disposed

> to indite
> Wars, . . . the only Argument
> Heroic deem'd, chief maistry to dissect
> With long and tedious havoc fabl'd Knights
> In Battles feign'd.
> (*Paradise Lost*, IX. 27–31)

Although he was determined "not to be negligently trained in the precepts of Christian religion,"[3] Milton evidently held "heroic men or famous cities" to be sufficiently "laudable things" and worthy of the best and most honorable effort and conduct that the aspiring poet could offer. Milton's emphasis here is not only on the suitability of the subject matter to be celebrated, but on the worthiness of the celebrant as well.

---

2. Hughes, *John Milton: Complete Poems and Major Prose*, p. 694.
3. *Ibid.*, pp. 694–95.

Such worthiness Milton understands, in addition to "the precepts of Christian religion," in terms of "those happy twins" of love's "divine generation": "knowledge and virtue"[4]—to be classically celebrated two years later in Milton's letter to Samuel Hartlib.

It is these same "happy twins" that inform the Preface to Book II of *The Reason of Church Government*, as is clear from the straightforward contrast that Milton draws between "the writings and interludes of libidinous and ignorant poetasters" and "the main consistence of a true poem, the choice of such persons as they ought to introduce, and what is moral and decent to each one."[5] However, Milton's understanding of the true import of knowledge and virtue is, in turn, informed by his recognition of the indispensability, for poetry and for the poet, of "the very critical art of composition"[6]—not in terms of lapping up "vicious principles in sweet pills to be swallowed down," but rather in terms of painting out and describing the holy and sublime, the amiable or grave, the passionate or admirable "with a solid and treatable smoothness."[7] In Milton's own words,

> all these things with a solid and treatable smoothness to paint out and describe. Teaching over the whole book of sanctity and virtue through all the instances of example, with such delight to those especially of soft and delicious temper who will not so much as look upon Truth herself, unless they see her elegantly dressed, that whereas the paths of honesty and good life appear now rugged and difficult, though they be indeed easy and pleasant, they would then appear to all men both easy and pleasant, though they were rugged and difficult indeed.[8]

---

4. *Ibid.*, p. 694.
5. *Ibid.*, p. 670.
6. *Ibid.*, p. 669.
7. *Ibid.*, p. 670.
8. *Ibid.*

Milton's primary concern with the "true poem" ("the composition and pattern of the best and honorablest things") is neither limited to methodology for its own sake nor restricted to the mere imposition of morality on his countrymen. Rather, it is centered in such a fusion of method and matter as would be of the greatest benefit, as he puts it, "to our youth and gentry"—and indeed "to all men." Milton is concerned with the *matter* of "Truth herself." However, he is equally concerned with the *method* of "teaching over the whole book of sanctity and virtue through *all* the instances of example,"[9] including not only "whatsoever in religion is holy and sublime, in virtue amiable or grave," but also

> whatsoever hath passion or admiration in all the changes of that which is called fortune from without, or the wily subtleties and refluxes of man's thoughts from within.[10]

Indeed, Milton's very concern with "those especially of soft and delicious temper," no less than his abhorrence of "the writings and interludes of libidinous and ignorant poetasters," attests to his regard for poetic propriety.

But the converse is also true. Milton's interest in "the very critical art of composition" that characterizes "those frequent songs throughout the law and prophets" hardly excludes his admiration for "their divine argument." Milton's theory of poetry is, in fact, concerned with the *fusion* of both "divine argument" and "the very critical art of composition," neither of which alone is of sufficient "power, *beside the office of a pulpit*, to inbreed and cherish in a great people the seeds of virtue and civility, to allay the perturbations of the mind, and set the affections in right tune."[11]Merritt Hughes is right that

9. Italics mine.
10. *Ibid.*, p. 670.
11. *Ibid.*, p. 669; italics mine.

Milton's concern with painting out and describing "all these things with a solid and treatable smoothness . . . . Teaching over the whole book of sanctity and virtue through all the instances of example" is a "classic statement of the Renaissance faith in virtue and learning as the foundation of the poetic character."[12]

Thus, any consideration of Milton's theory of poetry must, in the end, come back to the common denominator of the poet and poetry: "a true poem." In the case of the first, that is, of the poet, Milton clearly defines the source of the poet's competence and power. For the true poet, what is needed is a studious and untiring spirit, continuously motivated and sustained by divine inspiration. As Milton puts it, in connection with his pledge to produce in later years a work of major poetic significance,

> as being a work not to be raised from the heat of youth, or the vapors of wine, like that which flows at waste from the pen of some vulgar amorist, or the trencher fury of a riming parasite, nor to be obtained by the invocation of Dame Memory and her Siren daughters, but by devout prayer to that eternal Spirit who can enrich with all utterance and knowledge, and sends out his seraphim with the hallowed fire of his altar, to touch and purify the lips of whom he pleases. *To this must be added* industrious and select reading, steady observation, insight into all seemly and generous arts and affairs.[13]

The sequence, partly indicated here by the words in italics (to which I shall presently return), is crucial. However, for a correct understanding of the second element in "a true poem," that is, of poetry, we must now go to Milton's classic letter to Samuel Hartlib.

---

12. *Ibid.*, p. 670n.
13. *Ibid.*, p. 671; italics mine.

In his generally perceptive discussion of Milton's poetics, Christopher Grose appropriately commends Balachandra Rajan for the latter's "masterly exposition of 'Simple, Sensuous, and Passionate' [which] remains the most useful of the commentaries."[14] Grose correctly observes also that Milton's *Of Education* is his "most influential statement on poetry,"[15] and that "poetry does indeed bulk" large in Milton's scheme.[16] However, Grose apparently misses Rajan's succinct statement, toward the conclusion of Rajan's essay, of his major points:

> Through education, through virtue, we know God. We imitate Him and therefore His Creation. We return and approach to the Nature which is His Art. If Milton's epic programme is studied under these *dicta* we can see good reasons for his writing *Paradise Lost*.[17]

Rajan's point is well taken. Moreover, it is impossible to appreciate either Milton's poetics (as it is contained in the pertinent sections of his prose) or the application of his poetic theory to *Paradise Lost* without recognizing the essentially paradoxical nature of poetry in the total Miltonic scheme. What is much more important, however, is a correct understanding of the *reasons* for the paradox. Those reasons pervade Milton's discussion of poetry in *Of Education*.

Grose correctly notes that "Milton clearly accepts the traditional inner correlatives of the scale [the Great Chain of Being]; but its graduations are also associated with the limita-

---

14. Grose, p. 30. See also pp. 34 and 42.
15. *Ibid.*, p. 29.
16. *Ibid.*, p. 30.
17. "Simple, Sensuous and Passionate," *The Review of English Studies* 21 (1945): 289–301; reprinted in Arthur E. Barker, ed., *Milton: Modern Essays in Criticism* (New York: Oxford University Press, 1965), p. 14.

tions of fallen perception."[18] Grose also correctly supports his observation with the following quotation:

> But because our understanding cannot in this body found itself but on sensible things, nor arrive so clearly to the knowledge of God and things invisible, as by orderly conning over the visible and inferior creature, the same method is necessarily to be followed in all discreet teaching.

It is, however, at this point that Grose appears to misconstrue Milton's total intention in discussing the primary point contained in the preceding quotation—which, incidentally, is indeed quoted by Rajan, as Grose observes, but which comes, of course, from *Of Education*, and, in fact, from a context with which Grose does not directly deal.[19]

The last quotation above is immediately preceded in *Of Education* by an even more significant sentence—a statement that is surely among the most important that Milton has ever made regarding learning and virtue:

> The end then of learning is to repair the ruins of our first parents *by regaining to know God aright*, and out of that knowledge to love him, to imitate him, to be like him, as we may the nearest *by possessing our souls of true virtue*, which being united to the heavenly grace of faith makes up the highest perfection.[20]

This definition of the chief objective of education, which Douglas Bush rightly calls "the less familiar but even more

---

18. Grose, p. 30.
19. See *ibid.*, p. 31n; Rajan, p. 5; and Hughes, *John Milton: Complete Poems and Major Prose*, p. 631.
20. Hughes, *John Milton: Complete Poems and Major Prose*, p. 631; italics mine.

truly Miltonic one,"[21] clearly reinforces the chief emphases on learning and virtue in Milton's discussions of the poet and poetry in *An Apology for Smectymnuus* and *The Reason of Church Government*. The end of learning is the knowledge of God, and the best means of securing such knowledge is by our *imitation* of God through our love for Him and our continuous striving after true virtue. But we have a major problem, Milton suggests: "our understanding cannot in this body found itself but on sensible things." If we are, then, to "arrive . . . clearly to the knowledge of God and things invisible," we must do so within the categories of our own postlapsarian condition—that is, "by *orderly* conning over the visible and inferior creature."[22] Because these are the unavoidable circumstances of our fallen condition, Milton argues, "the same method [of arriving at things invisible through things visible] is necessarily to be followed in all discreet teaching." The program of studies outlined in Milton's tractate is precisely that "method," with exactly the same aim of arriving "clearly to the knowledge of God and things invisible."

This, in sum, is the inescapably paradoxical nature of the human condition, Milton realizes. Consequently, he quite appropriately places the organic arts, including poetry, at the end of the suggested program of studies. Crucial, however, for our correct understanding of Milton's concept of poetry in *Of Education* is an equally correct perception of his *apparent* equivocation in his definition and estimate of the importance of poetry. Here are Milton's own words:

> To which poetry would be made *subsequent, or indeed rather precedent*, as being less subtle and fine, but more simple, sensuous, and passionate. *I mean not here the prosody of a verse,*

---

21. "Religious and Ethical Principles," *"Paradise Lost" in Our Time* (Ithaca, N.Y.: Cornell University Press, 1945), pp. 29–57; reprinted in Barker, *Modern Essays in Criticism*, p. 159.
22. Italics mine.

which they could not but have hit on before among the
rudiments of grammar; *but that sublime art* which in
Aristotle's Poetics, in Horace, and the Italian commentaries
of Castelvetro, Tasso, Manzonni, and others, teaches what
the laws are of a true epic poem, what of a dramatic, what of
a lyric, what decorum is, which is the grand masterpiece to
observe. *This would make them soon perceive what despicable
creatures our common rhymers and play-writers be, and show them
what religious, what glorious and magnificent use might be made of
poetry, both in divine and human things.*[23]

The equivocation in Milton's "subsequent, or indeed rather
precedent" is, I submit, only apparent—not real. As Rajan
has observed,[24] poetry is, in Milton's understanding, both
subsequent *and* precedent to logic and rhetoric. Further, even
if Milton appears to speak here of poetry's "pedagogical
utility,"[25] his formulation is much more than merely interesting; it is crucial. What is interesting is the apparent inconsistency between Milton's suggested program of study in *Of
Education* (in which the organic arts, including poetry, are
placed at the climax of a rigorous period of training) and the
seemingly opposite emphasis in *The Reason of Church
Government* (in which several general categories of study *follow*
an obvious concern with, and commitment to, the sacred
office of poet). It is to such a dedication to "the knowledge of
God and things invisible" that the more mundane, though
necessary, pursuits "must be added."[26] Again, however, there
is, in fact, no inconsistency here. For such a dedication is
perfectly in keeping with the chief objective of all learning as it
is described in *Of Education*.

Poetry is "subsequent" in Milton's educational scheme because it requires the most thorough preparation in grammar,

23. Hughes, *John Milton: Complete Poems and Major Prose*, pp. 636–37; italics mine.
24. Rajan, p. 8.
25. Grose, p. 71.
26. Hughes, *John Milton: Complete Poems and Major Prose*, p. 671.

select readings, the industrial arts, politics, logic, and rhetoric. However, it is *precedent* precisely because it is "that sublime art" which "would . . . show them what religious, what glorious and magnificent use might be made of poetry, both in divine and human things"—that is to say, for the fullest achievement of the end of learning. But more than this, poetry is "precedent," "as being less subtle and fine" (than either logic or rhetoric) "but more simple, sensuous, and passionate," and therefore most capable of fully utilizing and articulating the only means available in man's fallen condition for the achievement of the knowledge of God and of true virtue: "orderly conning over the visible and inferior creature," "because our understanding cannot in this body found itself but on sensible things." Rajan has put the matter in memorable terms:

> We possess our souls of heavenly virtue not to escape, but to redeem our bodies: and at this point of emergence of knowledge into action the hierarchic values are reversed. We measure our understanding by its awareness of the changeless; we measure our utterance by its capacity to change. To say in this context that poetry is "more simple, sensuous and passionate" means that its transforming intelligence permeates even the frontiers of reality, that the security of a perfected understanding orders the scope and grandeur of its utterance.[27]

To put the matter in its simplest, yet fundamentally paradoxical and illogical, form: in Milton's poetics, poetry is both "subsequent" *and* "precedent" because the most effective *means* of learning is, finally, the very *end* of learning; and the very *end* of learning is, in terms of its most realistic fulfillment, its most effective *means*.

---

27. Rajan, p. 9.

ii

It is this circular, paradoxical characteristic of Milton's poetics that chiefly informs both the structure and the theme of *Paradise Lost*. As Dennis Burden correctly observes, Milton's use of literary theory as a fundamental part of the work of art "is a tactic common in Milton's poetry. Literary theory is always employed organically in it, setting up one of the controls under which the work develops."[28] Consequently, we may well expect to find at work in *Paradise Lost*—as indeed we do—this fundamental paradoxical characteristic of Milton's literary theory. As a matter of fact, it is especially in Milton's poetry that this element of his poetics works most effectively to bring together into a viable and dynamic poetic unity his rationalist sympathies, his humanist enlightenment, his neoclassical leanings, his biblical allusiveness, and his transcendent poetic vision. Rosalie Colie is quite right that "in paradox, form and content, subject and object are collapsed into one, in an ultimate insistence upon the unity of being. . . . One is forced to fuse categories, since paradox manifestly manages at once to be creative and critical, at once its own subject and its own object, turning endlessly in and upon itself."[29]

Paradise Lost turns endlessly "in and upon itself" because both the epic pattern and the biblical idea, both the poetic decorum and the transcendent vision work together in effective poetic unity to establish the central focus of the poem's world: the paradoxical nature of God's justice, actualized, from beginning to end, through the unique function of the Son. In *Paradise Lost*, it is God's justice, explicitly manifested in the person and function of the Son, that unifies the poem's

---

28. Dennis H. Burden, *The Logical Epic* (Cambridge, Mass.: Harvard University Press, 1967), p. 60.
29. Rosalie L. Colie, *Paradoxia Epidemica: The Renaissance Tradition of Paradox* (Princeton, N.J.: Princeton University Press, 1966), p. 518.

circular structure and its illogical insistence on the creative and restorative nature of God's ways.

Moreover, we seriously misunderstand such paradoxical complexity when we make the judgment that the poet failed to "justify the ways of God to men." Such a conclusion exhibits, it would appear, a sensibility grievously impaired by logical and discursive modes of thought. Logically and discursively, Milton proves nothing. For whatever predicative evidence he may be thought to have offered (by asserting eternal Providence in *Paradise Lost*) is continuously doubled back upon itself as subject with the disconcertingly tautological implication that Providence is providential and that justice is just. However, paradoxically and poetically, Milton "proves" everything he seeks to demonstrate in *Paradise Lost*. For through paradox and poetry, he is able to manipulate the formal and topical elements of epic not only in terms of a circular portrayal of providential Providence and of just justice, but more significantly, in terms of an imaginative identification of structure and theme, of form and content, of method and matter. But more than this, the imaginative identification is considerably heightened by a structural and thematic disposition that moves continuously and inescapably toward the central paradoxical significance of the Son. *Paradise Lost* turns endlessly "in and upon itself" because every significant feature of the epic pattern and of the biblical idea serves to define, and is simultaneously defined by, the unique person and function of the Son.

Of all the characters in the poem, the Son most effectively unifies the various elements of the poem's structure. By His paradoxical function in the poem, the Son activates and sustains the sweeping, circular movement that begins with God and ends in God. In every instance in which He appears in *Paradise Lost*, the Son functions to reinforce the essentially creative and restorative nature of God's justice. For example,

in Raphael's admonitory conversation with Adam in Books
V – VIII, which Joseph Summers perceptively calls the "pattern at the centre,"[30] not only do the two significant episodes,
the War in Heaven and the Creation, clearly depend upon the
decisive action of the Son, but the Son functions paradoxically
as a rather unique repository of both avenging justice and
creative vitality. As He declares, after being entrusted by the
Father with the task of routing the rebellious Host,

> whom thou hat'st, I hate, *and can put on*
> *Thy terror, as I put thy mildness on,*
> Image of thee in all things.
>
> (VI. 734–36)[31]

The paradoxical capability of the Son is clear. Moreover, in
the total action that follows—that is, the conclusion of the
War in Heaven and the Creation—the Son exemplifies this
double capacity in His terrifying routing of the rebellious
angels and in His serene, majestic movement through the
specific phases of the Creation. " . . . stand only and
behold / God's indignation on these Godless pour'd / By mee"
(VI. 810–12), He remarks to the faithful angels. And the
narrative voice graphically depicts the Son's terrifying
countenance as He prepares to engage the rebels:

> So spake the Son, and into terror chang'd
> His count'nance too severe to be beheld
> And full of wrath bent on his Enemies.
>
> (VI. 824–26)

In appropriate contrast to such terror, the Son's majestic

---

30. Joseph H. Summers, *The Muse's Method: An Introduction to 'Paradise Lost'*
(Cambridge, Mass.: Harvard University Press, 1962), chapter 5; reprinted in C. A.
Patrides, ed., *Milton's Epic Poetry: Essays on 'Paradise Lost' and 'Paradise Regained'*
(Middlesex, England: Penguin Books, Ltd., 1967), pp. 179–214.
31. Italics mine.

serenity is superbly portrayed by the poet as the Son readies
Himself for His "great Expedition" into the turbulence of
Chaos:

> Meanwhile the Son
> On his great Expedition now appear'd,
> Girt with Omnipotence, with Radiance crown'd
> Of Majesty Divine, Sapience and Love
> Immense, and all his Father in him shone.
>
> (VII. 192–96)

No less beautiful and serene is the Son's sovereign control of
"the vast immeasurable Abyss" of Chaos:

> On Heav'nly ground they stood, and from the shore
> They view'd the vast immeasurable Abyss
> Outrageous as a Sea, dark, wasteful, wild,
> Up from the bottom turn'd by furious winds
> And surging waves, as Mountains to assault
> Heav'n's highth, and with the Centre mix the Pole.
>   Silence, ye troubl'd waves, and thou Deep, peace,
> Said then th' Omnific Word, your discord end:
>   Nor stay'd, but on the Wings of Cherubim
> Uplifted, in Paternal Glory rode
> Far into *Chaos*, and the World unborn;
> For *Chaos* heard his voice: him all his Train
> Follow'd in bright procession to behold
> Creation, and the wonders of his might.
>
> (VII. 210–23)

However, as important as the Son's paradoxical capacity for
both terror and serenity, both hatred and love, both avenging
justice and creative order is His fundamental function of reinforcing the creative and restorative nature of God's justice
through that very paradoxical capability. For what really
matters, in the final analysis, is the poet's imaginative identification of the Son with both the avenging justice over evil
and the creative and restorative processes of the poem's

world—that is, with the Son's fundamental function as the poem's coordinating structural and thematic principle. It is exactly this implicit poetic effect (in addition to the explicitly stated purpose of his admonitory conversation with Adam) that Raphael's narrative achieves in these central books of *Paradise Lost*. Through his sensitive manipulation of the Son's paradoxical capacity, Milton is able to establish not only a definitive relationship between the Son's avenging justice and His creative agency, but also an indispensable focus on the creative and restorative nature of the divine ways.

In the context of Raphael's narrative, Adam (and, indeed, the reader) must learn to recognize not only the wickedness of evil and the desirability of goodness (and surely, not merely the divine sanction against apostasy and the divine endorsement of obedience and loyalty), but, more important, the significant relationship between God's justice and the creative purposes of the divine ways uniquely exemplified in the paradoxical person and function of the Son. Thus, to Adam's perceptive query:

> what cause
> Mov'd the Creator in his holy Rest
> Through all Eternity so late to build
> In *Chaos* . . . ,
>
> (VII. 90–93)

Raphael introduces the entire account of the Creation with a clear emphasis on the definitive connection between the just consequences of Satan's apostasy and the creative purposes of the divine ways, in VII. 131–91, where the concluding lines describing the angelic chorus in Heaven unequivocally reinforce the entire point:

> Glory to him whose just avenging ire
> Had driven out th' ungodly from his sight
> And th' habitations of the just; to him

Glory and praise, whose wisdom had ordain'd
Good out of evil to create, instead
Of Spirits malign a better Race to bring
Into their vacant room, and thence diffuse
His good to Worlds and Ages infinite.
                                                (VII. 184–91)[32]

"Good out of evil to *create*" clearly links such restorative purposes to the glorious action of the "just avenging ire"—an
action that is not only understood by the angels to be *just*, but
that is also implicitly *restorative*, and thus, itself essentially
creative. When, upon the completion of the Creation, we find
the angels once again celebrating the glorious event in song,
we are not surprised either at their repeated allusion to the
inglorious failure of the rebellious action against Heaven's
"mighty King" or at their reiteration of the cause which
"Mov'd the Creator . . . so late to build / In *Chaos*":

Great are thy works, *Jehovah*, infinite
Thy power; what thought can measure thee or tongue
Relate thee; *greater now in thy return*
Than from the Giant Angels; thee that day
Thy Thunders magnifi'd; but *to create*
Is greater than created to destroy.
Who can impair thee, mighty King, or bound
Thy Empire? easily the proud attempt
Of Spirits apostate and thir Counsels vain
Thou hast repell'd, while impiously they thought
Thee to diminish, and from thee withdraw
The number of thy worshippers. Who seeks
To lessen thee, against his purpose serves
To manifest the more thy might: his evil
Thou usest, and from thence creat'st more good.
                                                (VII. 602–16)[33]

---

32. Italics mine.
33. Italics mine.

A new, explicit note—it should be observed—has entered the angelic song: "to create / Is greater than created to destroy." In fact, as Raphael has already informed Adam, the Son's pursuit of the rebellious Host did not end in their destruction. "Eternal wrath / Burn'd after them to the bottomless pit" (VI. 865–66). However,

> half his strength he put not forth, but check'd
> His Thunder in mid Volley, *for he meant*
> *Not to destroy*, but root them out of Heav'n.
>   (VI. 853–55)[34]

That the angels would, nevertheless, include such a thought in their appropriate paean appears to indicate the considerable significance they attach to the positive action of *creating*. Consequently, they fittingly regard the Son as greater now (in His return from His creation of the universe) "than [He was when He returned] from the Giant Angels" (on the day of their ignominious routing by the Son as God's avenging justice).

Clearly, the emphasis in this concluding song of praise, even more than in the introductory paean to God's creative goodness, is intended by the poet (and imaginatively, by Raphael) to reinforce the essential purpose of the Son's paradoxical function both as God's avenging justice and as the chief instrument of the divine creative goodness. That purpose, emphatically reiterated in this concluding angelic hymn, is the unequivocally creative and restorative nature of the divine ways, including even the divine justice, as the Son's decision "not to destroy" (even in His role as God's avenging justice) helps to confirm. Evidently, the Son realizes, as do the Angels, that "to create / Is greater than created to destroy."

Rosalie Colie correctly suggests that "Milton's preoccupation with the Creation in *Paradise Lost* is quite obvious; from

---

34. Italics mine.

beginning to end the poem refers to creation, creativity, and re-creation."[35] Equally true is the fact that the Son stands uniquely at the center of this emphasis in *Paradise Lost*, as He so unmistakably does in the poem's central books (Books V – VIII). What is even more important is that the Son's central position in the creative and restorative processes of the poem's world invariably includes His paradoxical function as God's justice and as the chief instrument of God's creative purposes — suggesting both the complexity of the creative and restorative processes and the Son's significant stylistic function as the chief structural principle of *Paradise Lost*. To put the matter another way: without this paradoxical capability (with its continuous reciprocal effect on the two basic elements of the paradox), the Son would function merely as the instrument either of God's justice or of God's creative and restorative purposes, but hardly as both; or, if we are willing to grant that, hardly as both *simultaneously;* or if, further, we are willing to grant that, hardly in that paradoxical sense which invests either capacity with the essential qualities of the other. That is to say, even if we are willing to grant that in *Paradise Lost* the Son functions at the same time as the instrument both of God's justice and of God's creative and restorative purposes, He could hardly be said to function as the chief coordinating structural principle of *Paradise Lost* without that fundamental paradoxical capability which we have seen at work in the poem's central books. For without that unique paradoxical capacity, the Son could neither exemplify, as He does, the essentially creative and restorative nature of God's *justice* and the *complexity* (including the requisite loyalty of the creature) of God's creative and restorative purposes; nor could He unify, as He also does, the poem's various structural elements (including the epic pattern and the biblical idea) into a non-

---

35. Colie, p. 182.

linear, circular movement chiefly characterized by a continuous focus "in and upon itself."

Evidence of this type of unity is everywhere in *Paradise Lost*.
We find it in Satan's ironic recovery in Book I, for example,
where the rhetoric and the imagery serve indeed to build up
the fallen archangel to magnificently heroic proportions, but
do so in an ultimately dubious context in which, for one thing,
Satan himself recognizes the essentially creative and restorative nature of God's providence (I, 162–65), and where Satan,
as the narrative voice explains,

>   nor ever thence
> Had ris'n or heav'd his head, but that the will
> And high permission of all-ruling Heaven
> Left him at large to his own dark designs,
> That with reiterated crimes he might
> Heap on himself damnation, while he sought
> Evil to others, and enrag'd might see
> How all his malice serv'd but to bring forth
> Infinite goodness, grace and mercy shown
> On Man by him seduc't, but on himself
> Treble confusion, wrath and vengeance pour'd.
>   (I. 210–20)

Similar evidence abounds in Book II, during the debate in
Pandaemonium, for example, where the irony of the language
and the action is shrewdly developed by the poet with a subtle
but relentless energy—from Moloch's spurious observation
(II. 75–77), through Belial's basically true, but manipulative,
perception (II. 190–93) and Mammon's delusion (II. 269–70),
to Beelzebub's essentially accurate reproof (II. 377–78), in
which, however, he ironically fails to include his most recent
proposal, "first devis'd / By *Satan*, and in part propos'd" (II.
379–80). As the narrative voice suitably remarks,

>   for whence,
> But from the Author of all ill could Spring

So deep a malice, to confound the race
Of mankind in one root, and Earth with Hell
To mingle and involve, done all to spite
The great Creator? *But thir spite still serves
His glory to augment.*

(II. 380–86)[36]

Equally copious evidence of this type of unity in *Paradise Lost* may be found elsewhere in the poem, especially in those sections where the poet has portrayed the assault of evil upon the divine creative goodness. The obvious example of this is, of course, Satan's successful temptation of Eve, which results in the Fall of the human pair (in Book IX), but also (through God's restorative goodness) in their repentance and restoration (in Book X)—with the appropriate sequel of Michael's extensive education of Adam in Books XI and XII. To Satan, the "One fatal Tree . . . / Forbidden them to taste" (IV. 514–15) is, as he decides during his first assault upon Eden, a

fair foundation laid whereon to build
Thir ruin!

(IV. 521–22)

And the poet encourages the implications of the phrase, "Thir ruin," through his poetic exemplification (in Book IX)

Of Man's First Disobedience, and the Fruit
Of that Forbidden Tree, whose mortal taste
Brought Death into the World, and all our woe,
With loss of *Eden,*

(I. 1–4)

precisely because he is developing a structural unity that is characterized chiefly by a paradoxical complexity which, in

---

36. Italics mine.

turn, demands the thematic reality of a genuine loss of
Paradise as a crucial element of that incipient paradox:

> So saying, her rash hand in evil hour
> Forth reaching to the Fruit, she pluck'd, she eat:
> Earth felt the wound, and Nature from her seat
> Sighing through all her Works gave signs of woe,
> *That all was lost.*
>
> (IX. 780–84)[37]

Equally necessary for the viable function of the paradoxical
structure, however, is the second crucial element of the incipient paradox—already expressed by the poet in appropriately restorative terms in the initial invocation:

> till one greater Man
> Restore us, and regain the blissful Seat.
>
> (I. 4–5)

In *Paradise Lost*, that "one greater Man" is surely the Son, as
the poet makes clear in the remaining books of the epic, which
follow Book IX, the book of the Fall. For example, at the
conclusion of the judgment of Adam and Eve (in Book X) by
the Son,

> Man's Friend, his Mediator, his design'd
> *Both Ransom and Redeemer voluntary,*
>
> (X. 60–61)[38]

the narrative voice explains:

> So judg'd he Man, *both Judge and Savior sent.*
>
> (X. 209)[39]

---

37. Italics mine.
38. Italics mine.
39. Italics mine.

The Son's obvious paradoxical function expressed here
confirms, moreover, His stated intention regarding the nature
of His impending judgment of Adam and Eve:

> yet I shall temper so
> Justice with Mercy, as may illustrate most
> Them fully satisfied, and thee appease.
>
> (X. 77–79)

Here, in very concise terms, is the fundamentally reciprocal
effect of the Son's paradoxical function (as "both Judge and
Savior," as "both Ransom and Redeemer voluntary") that pervades the whole of *Paradise Lost*.

The restorative characteristic of the tempered judgment of
Adam and Eve by the Son stands in direct contrast to both the
tentative judgment of Satan by the Son in Book X and
Michael's unequivocal references (in Books XI and XII) to
Satan's final defeat by the Son as the risen Christ. This is as it
should be, since the defeat of evil in *Paradise Lost* is vital to the
unity and coherence of the poem's structural scheme. More
significantly, the defeat of Satanic evil, depicted in these closing books of *Paradise Lost*, serves both to reinforce the Son's
unique paradoxical function in the poem and to exemplify—
with graphic, poetic accuracy—the germinative irony and
paradox which, as we have seen, pervade the language and the
action of Satan and his fallen angels in Books I and II.

Satan is well aware that the Son is the "destin'd restorer of
Mankind" (X. 646). As he reports to the fallen Host upon his
return to Hell after his successful temptation of Eve (and
Adam),

> that which to mee belongs
> Is enmity, which he will put between

> Mee and Mankind; I am to bruise his heel;
> His Seed, when is not yet, shall bruise my head.
> (X. 496–99)

Although he tries (X. 500–501) to preserve the lighthearted mood of his remark in X. 485–90, he is, in fact, terrified of the presence of the Son of God, as his action upon the recent descent of the Son from Heaven to judge the human pair indicates:

> but when he saw descend
> The Son of God to judge them, terrifi'd
> Hee fled, not hoping to escape, but shun
> The present, fearing guilty what his wrath
> Might suddenly inflict.
> (X. 337–41)

From what we already know about the essentially restorative judgment of Adam and Eve by the Son (X. 55–228), the juxtaposition here of the Son's descent "to judge them" and Satan's terrified flight is yet another enacted testimony to the Son's paradoxical function as "both Judge and Savior," the "destin'd restorer of Mankind."

A similar juxtaposition, with a similar point, informs Michael's entire revelatory visit with Adam in Books XI and XII, as indicated, for example, in the poet's significant description of the ascent of Michael and Adam to the Hill of Paradise—a passage too frequently overlooked in discussions of these closing books of the poem:

> So both ascend
> In the Visions of God: It was a Hill
> Of Paradise the highest, from whose top
> The Hemisphere of Earth in clearest Ken
> Stretcht out to the amplest reach of prospect lay.

> Not higher that Hill nor wider looking round,
> Whereon *for different cause* the Tempter set
> Our second *Adam* in the Wilderness,
> To show him all Earth's Kingdoms and thir Glory.
>   (XI. 376–84)[40]

The *cause* for which Michael invites Adam to ascend the Hill
of Paradise is different from the Tempter's cause, for Michael
has been sent, as the Father plainly instructs him, to

>   reveal
> To Adam what shall come in future days,
> As I shall thee enlighten, *intermix*
> *My Cov'nant in the woman's seed renew'd;*
> So send them forth, though sorrowing, yet in peace.
>   (XI. 113–17)[41]

And the very last words spoken in the poem, by Eve, make
precisely the same point:

> This further consolation yet secure
> I carry hence; though *all* by mee is *lost*,
> Such favor I unworthy am voutsaf't,
> By mee the Promis'd Seed shall *all restore*.
>   (XII. 620–23)[42]

It is surely not difficult to see the poet's juxtaposition here of
"all . . . lost" and "all restore," nor the obvious similarity between Eve's concluding comment and the Father's introductory command to Michael (XI. 113–17), nor, what is more
important, the clear connection between this paradoxical emphasis and the inherent paradox with which the first five lines
of the poem vibrate. Moreover, everything that occurs be-

---

40. Italics mine.
41. Italics mine.
42. Italics mine.

tween the Father's direction to Michael and Eve's final remark—indeed, the whole of *Paradise Lost*—is invested by the poet with a resounding affirmation of the Son's unique function as the creative and restorative justice of God. It is this fact, more than anything else, that provides the unity and coherence of *Paradise Lost*, poetically delineating the circular structural movement—from the initial invocation to Eve's concluding consolatory remark and back again to the central books of the poem (Books V–VIII), where, rather than with the epic beginning *in medias res*, the primary events of the action of the poem, in fact, begin. It is from this beginning that the poem's fundamental pattern radiates outward to every significant thematic and structural detail, even as every important thematic and structural element unavoidably focuses inward upon the central and inescapable presence of the Son.

This is exactly the aim of Michael's revelatory mission to Adam in Books XI and XII, as Adam's classic commentary on his own vision, in the midst of "the Visions of God," clearly indicates:

> O goodness infinite, goodness immense!
> That all this good of evil shall produce,
> And evil turn to good; more wonderful
> Than that which by creation first brought forth
> Light out of darkness!
> (XII. 469–73)

Significantly, Adam associates God's bringing good out of evil (through the unique function of the Son as God's restorative justice) with the previously narrated lesson of the Creation (characterized, in the context of Raphael's total narrative, by exactly this emphasis on God's restorative justice). For Adam, in his own instructive juxtaposition of the two most important lessons he has learned (from his two angelic teachers), finally comes to realize that the "pattern at the centre" is germinally the pattern of the whole, in both of which—in characteristic paradoxical fashion—the "Judge and Savior sent" is no other than the "destin'd restorer of Mankind."

iii

In a generally forgotten discussion of "The Deification of Reason" in *Paradise Lost*, Charles Williams perceptively suggests that

> Heaven's glory climbs . . . to its climax in God, in its own state of unbegotten Reason and Power and Beauty, and that climax involves the imagination of its own entire submission to itself. *The full deific initiative of heaven Milton could hardly present; heaven for him had to know itself perfectly to some point short of that. It must then willingly abandon itself only to find that it realizes itself utterly so. Paradise Lost* is a poem of its own kind, . . . [and] we can all add to the list of local materializations which we may find it difficult to accept. *But the materialization is a necessity of the poem, and we have to accept it because otherwise we cannot have the poem.* [43]

Although he does not develop this crucial observation, Williams pinpoints, in this comment, the stylistic crux of *Paradise Lost*. For not only does he recognize the poem's circular, paradoxical movement in what he calls "the imagination of its own entire submission to itself" and in his suggestion that heaven "must then willingly abandon itself only to find that it realizes itself utterly so," but he correctly emphasizes the necessity in *Paradise Lost* for a "materialization" through which alone we are able, in the first place, to "have the poem," and also to apprehend even Heaven's "own state of unbegotten Reason and Power and Beauty." This, as we have seen, is

---

43. *Reason and Beauty in the Poetic Mind* (London: Oxford University Press, 1933), p. 125; italics mine.

exactly Milton's point in *Of Education*, not only in the apparent ambivalence of poetry's being "subsequent, or indeed rather precedent," but especially in his insistence that, as quoted before,

> because our understanding cannot in this body found itself but on sensible things, nor arrive so clearly to the knowledge of God and things invisible as by orderly conning over the visible and inferior creature, the same method is necessarily to be followed in all discreet teaching.

Concerned, as he should be, with "teaching over the whole book of sanctity and virtue through all the instances of example," the practicing poet—for Milton—must be able both to recognize poetry's circular and paradoxical import and to exemplify that poetic crux in his art, if that art is effectively to incorporate the "method . . . necessarily to be followed" in arriving "clearly to the knowledge of God and things invisible"—"because our understanding cannot in this body found itself but on sensible things."

These are exactly the poetic criteria that inform *Paradise Lost* where the indispensable imagery fuses appropriately with the poem's circular, paradoxical pattern to exemplify in *sensible* terms the poet's vision of "the knowledge of God and things invisible." In this sense, the entire poem is a complex simile (or metaphor, if you will) of the knowledge of God and things invisible. Moreover, we can still approach *Paradise Lost* (as we usually insist on doing) with a critical eye on Miltonic intention. That intention, when all—on both sides of the issue—is said and done, is Milton's explicit objective to "assert Eternal Providence, / And justify the ways of God to men" (I. 25–26)—an objective that is directly engaged by the poet in the pertinent and crucially placed invocations, but that is also indirectly enacted throughout *Paradise Lost*.

Milton's intention is expertly demonstrated, for example, in

Raphael's chosen method of presentation to Adam in V. 571–76:

> what surmounts the reach
> Of human sense, I shall delineate so,
> By lik'ning spiritual to corporal forms,
> As may express them best, though what if Earth
> Be but the shadow of Heav'n, and things therein
> Each to other like, more than on Earth is thought?

In terms both of "the knowledge of God and things invisible" and the method most requisite for arriving at such knowledge, Raphael's tutorial approach to Adam is clearly Milton's approach to the reader of his poem, and Raphael's demonstration of his chosen method (in his narration of the War in Heaven and of the Creation) is none other than Milton's poetic exemplification of the crux of his poetics—an important fact that, *in terms of the chief characteristics of Milton's poetics*, we too often forget.

Further, Raphael's tutorial method and Milton's exemplification of the crux of his poetics are the result not of some whimsical choice, but are ultimately determined by the very ontological constitution of the universe of *Paradise Lost*. In that world, as Raphael carefully explains to Adam (and Milton to us), the assertion of eternal Providence is inseparable both from the circular, paradoxical pattern that characterizes all significant movement in the poem's world and from the vital, unifying force of reason which, for the Soul, "is her being, / Discursive, or Intuitive" (V. 486–88). As Raphael explains to Adam,

> *one Almighty is, from whom*
> *All things proceed, and up to him return,*
> *If not deprav'd from good, created all*
> *Such to perfection, . . .*

> . . . So from the root
> Springs lighter the green stalk, from thence the leaves
> More aery, last the bright consummate flow'r
> Spirits odorous breathes: flow'rs and thir fruit
> Man's nourishment, by gradual scale sublim'd
> To vital spirits aspire, to animal,
> To intellectual, give both life and sense,
> Fancy and understanding, *whence the Soul*
> *Reason receives, and reason is her being,*
> *Discursive, or Intuitive; discourse*
> *Is oftest yours, the latter most is ours,*
> *Differing but in degree, of kind the same.*
> (V. 469–72, 479–90)[44]

Whether we choose to interpret these lines (as also the later passage in V. 571–76) in a Neoplatonic sense or, as William Madsen has taught us to see them, in terms of an essentially biblical typological symbolism, the thrust of Raphael's remarks in both passages inescapably stresses "a relationship between earth and heaven, between the physical and the spiritual, which is inherent in the nature of things."[45] In terms of the ontological unity of the poem's world, the chief characteristic of that relationship, I would suggest, is reason, which the Soul receives and which "*is her being,* / Discursive, or Intuitive."[46]

To misunderstand this cardinal principle of the poem's world is to misunderstand both God's justice and the poet's style in *Paradise Lost*. For reason—that is, "right reason," and not merely logic or rhetoric[47]—which, for the entire poem, as for all the characters of *Paradise Lost*, "is her being," finds its

---

44. Italics mine.
45. William G. Madsen, "Earth the Shadow of Heaven: Typological Symbolism in *Paradise Lost*," *PMLA* 75 (1960): 519–26; reprinted in Barker, *Milton: Modern Essays in Criticism*, p. 246.
46. Italics mine.
47. For a perceptive discussion of *recta ratio*, see Bush, pp. 161–68.

most effective expression in the central person and function of
the Son, who establishes the poem's essential frame of reference by unifying the various thematic and stylistic features
into a viable poetic whole. Thus, the Son is able to function,
throughout the poem, as its most effective Example—in a
world where "reason also is choice" (III. 108); where those
who violate its established ethos

> reason for thir Law refuse,
> Right reason for thir Law, and for thir King
> *Messiah* who by right of merit Reigns;
>
> (VI. 41–43)

and where, by thus violating the very essence of their being,
they prostitute "true Liberty" (XII. 83),

> which always with right Reason dwells
> Twinn'd, and from her hath no dividual being.
>
> (XII. 84–85)

In the end, it is this indispensable identification of reason
and freedom that best distinguishes reason from the "con-
tracted palm" of logic and from the "graceful and ornate"
rhetoric in *Paradise Lost*, enabling reason to transcend both the
circumscription of logic and the artificiality of rhetoric.[48] It is
this significant difference that characterizes all the distinctions
between the portraits of Satan (throughout the poem), of the
fallen angels, including Sin and Death (in Books I, II and X),
and of Adam and Eve immediately after the Fall (in IX.
1027–1189; X, 97–143; and X. 715–909), on the one hand,
and on the other, those of the angelic choruses, of the angelic
teachers, of the Son, of the Father, and even of the narrative
voice itself. Satan, for example, willingly commits himself to a

---

48. See Hughes, *John Milton: Complete Poems and Major Prose*, p. 636n.

crippling exchange of "true Liberty" (and so, true reason) for
an ironic heroism; a restorative allegiance to the creative
efficacy of the Son for a destructive loyalty to himself; and,
what is more significant, a "procéss of speech" (VII. 178) that
is not only "simple, sensuous, and passionate," but also "less
subtle and fine" than logic and rhetoric (clearly defining "what
glorious and magnificent use might be made of poetry, both in
divine and in human things")[49] for an impaired grandiloquence
which, however "simple, sensuous, and passionate" *per se*, is
incipiently ironic and explicitly parodic in its relation to that
"procéss of speech" which characterizes the creative and restorative processes of the poem's world. To put the matter
another way: it is *not* the fallen condition of the poem's
"procéss of speech" in contrast to "the real poem" that pro-
duces the "paradoxical tension" of *Paradise Lost*.[50] Rather, it is
the potentiality (latent in that poetically unavoidable process)
for both creation and destruction, both the full exercise of
rational liberty and the despotic enthrallment to self, that
gives the poem its tension, delineating and reinforcing the
paradoxical nature of that process through the continuous
pressure, in the poem's world, for enlightened choice. A
single, major example will have to suffice: the poet's portrayal
of Heaven in Book III.

Balachandra Rajan reminds us that "the language of *Paradise
Lost* works in conjunction with its structure and it is the union
of the two which we ought to be discussing when we use that
misleading label 'style.' "[51] And C. A. Patrides brings the
matter closer to our immediate concerns when, in discussing
the Father in Book III, he observes that "even the generally
decried forensic terms . . . explode far beyond Book III to

---

49. *Ibid.*, p. 637.
50. See Grose, p. 262.
51. "Introduction" to *Milton's Paradise Lost: Books I and II* (New York: Asia Publishing House, 1964), pp. xix–xxxviii; reprinted in Patrides, *Milton's Epic Poetry*, p. 287.

affect the entire structure of *Paradise Lost.*"⁵² Both Rajan and Patrides are right, and we do both *Paradise Lost* and its God a serious disservice either to separate the language of the poem from its structure or to define the nature of the God of *Paradise Lost* in terms of a linear and logical progression of the narrative. The fact is that all discussions of the Council in Heaven in Book III are inadequate that fail to consider the God of *Paradise Lost* in terms of the poem's paradoxical structure *and* language.

Equally inadequate are those discussions which see only the most superficial connection between the invocation at the beginning of Book III and the poet's presentation of the Heavenly Council that immediately follows. Like the "pattern at the centre" (in Books V – VIII), this equally important first half of Book III is characterized by a circular and paradoxical movement, which helps to delineate the similar movement of the entire poem. That is, the invocation and the Heavenly Council in Book III are simply another of Milton's specific poetic attempts to portray "a composition and pattern of the best and honorablest things" from "the whole book of sanctity and virtue" through still another *instance of example.* In fact, "example" is the most appropriate term for what the poet represents in this section of the poem. For this section of *Paradise Lost* is a perfect *example* not only of the true meaning of God's justice,⁵³ but also of the paradoxical style of the entire poem.

When, toward the conclusion of the angelic paean, the poet imaginatively participates in the choric address to the Son, exuberantly confessing:

---

52. See "*Paradise Lost* and the Language of Theology" in Ronald David Emma and John T. Shawcross, eds., *Language and Style in Milton: A Symposium in Honor of the Tercentenary of Paradise Lost* (New York: Frederick Ungar Publishing Co., Inc., 1967), p. 111.
53. See chapter 5, section ii of this study for a discussion of the poet's dramatization in Book III of the true meaning of God's justice in *Paradise Lost.*

                            thy Name
Shall be the copious matter of my Song
Henceforth, and never shall my Harp thy praise
Forget, nor from thy Father's praise disjoin,
                                        (III. 412–15)

it is not at all difficult to recognize the circular structure of the
episode, in which the concluding "Hail Son of God, Savior of
Men" (III. 412) is linked with the very first phrase of Book III,
"Hail holy Light" (III. 1). Moreover, whether or not we are
disposed to accept the "Light" invoked by the poet (III. 1) as
the "Son of God," it is clear that by the concluding choric
address the "Son of God" has become the "Light" of God—on
the evidence of the description of the Son both by the poet
(III. 138–40) and by the angelic choir (III. 384–88). Thus, the
dominant image (or perhaps symbol) of the invocation, pas-
sionately modulated through a variety of tonal turns (III.
21–26, 32–36, 40–46, 50, and 51–55), gradually actualizes
itself in the person of the Son of God as the *Light* of God.
Indeed, the circular movement, begun with the invocation and
brought to a close in the poet's imaginative stance at the
episode's end, has its magnetic center in none other than the
Father, who is portrayed as the very "Fountain of Light" (III.
375)—an attribute that is celebrated by the poet in some of the
most impressive lines in the whole of *Paradise Lost:*

                        thyself invisible
Amidst the glorious brightness where thou sit'st
Thron'd inaccessible, but when thou shad'st
The full blaze of thy beams, and through a cloud
Drawn round about thee like a radiant Shrine,
Dark with excessive bright thy skirts appear,
Yet dazzle Heav'n, that brightest Seraphim
Approach not, but with both wings veil their eyes.
                                        (III. 375–82)

Yet, it is the Son who, as the "Divine Similitude" (III. 384), best actualizes the Father's inaccessibility. For the Son functions, in the episode's circular pattern, as the motive structural force both from the center of Light to the circumference of actualized glory, and from the angels' virtually liturgical recognition of that glory back to the poet's stated objective in the invocation to "see and tell / Of things invisible to mortal sight" (III. 54–55) and forward again (as it were) to "th' Almighty Father" (III. 386)—that is, to "th' effulgence of his Glory" (III. 388) and, most significantly, to "his ample Spirit" which "rests," "transfus'd" upon the Son (III. 389).[54] To put the matter quite simply: as the actualization of the inaccessible Father, the Son functions as the repository not merely of the Father's Light, but also of His creative and restorative "Spirit."

This is precisely the point of the angels' hymn to the Son, in which their celebration of His visible brightness proceeds effortlessly to the wonder of His creative and restorative might, then, just as gently, moves into the crux of the entire episode, which they had, with great wonder, just witnessed: *the Son's voluntary offer to die for Man.* Milton develops the entire passage with subtle poetic skill:

> Thee next they sang of all Creation first,
> Begotten Son, Divine Similitude,
> In whose conspicuous count'nance, without cloud
> Made visible, th' Almighty Father shines,
> Whom else no Creature can behold, *on thee
> Impresst the effulgence of his Glory shines,
> Transfus'd on thee his ample Spirit rests.*

---

54. I agree with Merritt Hughes, who agrees with Maurice Kelley, that here and in VII. 165 and 209 (if not as clearly in I. 17 and VII. 235) "the reference is to the 'virtue and power of God the Father,' and 'not to the Third Person' or Holy Spirit." See Hughes, *John Milton: Complete Poems and Major Prose,* p. 267n. Cf. Maurice Kelley, *This Great Argument: Milton's De Doctrina Christiana as a Gloss upon Paradise Lost* (Princeton, N.J.: Princeton University Press, 1941), p. 109.

> *Hee Heav'n of Heavens and all the Powers therein*
> *By thee created, and by thee threw down*
> *Th' aspiring Dominations: . . .*
> Back from pursuit thy Powers with loud acclaim
> Thee only extoll'd, Son of thy Father's might,
> *To execute fierce vengeance on his foes:*
> *Not so on Man; him through their malice fall'n,*
> Father of Mercy and Grace, thou didst not doom
> So strictly, but much more to pity incline:
> *No sooner did thy dear and only Son*
> *Perceive thee purpos'd not to doom frail Man*
> So strictly, but much more to pity inclin'd,
> Hee to appease thy wrath, and end the strife
> Of Mercy and Justice in thy face discern'd,
> *Regardless of the Bliss wherein hee sat*
> Second to thee, *offer'd himself to die*
> *For man's offense.*
>
> (III. 383–410)[55]

It is at this point that the poet becomes the poet-celebrant, joining the concluding strains of the choric song with his own "Song / Henceforth" (III. 413–14) and pledging to memorialize the Son (and the Father) in continuous praise.

The poet-celebrant's pledge of continued devotion is clearly predicated upon the ecstatic acclaim that he accords the Son:

> O unexampl'd love,
> Love nowhere to be found less than Divine!
>
> (III. 410–11)

Yet, neither the effusive feeling of these lines nor the poet's visionary participation in the scene should cause us to overlook the meaning of what he is saying here. For despite the heightened tone and the visionary stance, the meaning is clearly dependent not only on the thrust of the immediate context

---

55. Italics mine.

(that is, the choric celebration of the Son), but especially on the pattern of the entire episode as it has emerged in the language and the action of the total scene. Conversely, the pattern of the entire episode, in terms of the language and the action, is itself defined by the nature and meaning of this final note of commendation, the crux of the choric song.

However liturgical and visionary the effect here, the emphasis is on the Son's unique, restorative function as the "Savior of Men." It is for *this* reason that the poet participates in the choric tribute, offering his "Song" and his "Harp" for the continuous celebration of the Son's *Name*, a name that he has already ascribed to the Son: "unexampl'd love." Yet, the name itself is ambivalent, or more accurately, paradoxical, since the very reason for celebrating the "Name" of the Son as "unexampl'd love" is that His unprecedented and incomparable love *is* exemplary. This, in the most concise terms, is ultimately the very point of the entire episode.

Central to the *exemplary* expression of the Son's "unexampl'd love" is the drama of choice so effectively portrayed by the poet in what is perhaps the most pregnant silence in all English literature:

> Dwells in all Heaven charity so dear?
> *He ask'd, but all the Heav'nly Choir stood mute,*
> *And silence was in Heav'n:* on man's behalf
> Patron or Intercessor none appear'd,
> Much less that durst upon his own head draw
> The deadly forfeiture, and ransom set.
>
> (III. 216–21)[56]

When we next hear about the angels, they are still in their state of astonished silence, though now their wonder is at the

---

56. Italics mine.

enormity of the Son's unprecedented willingness "as a sacrifice
/ Glad to be offer'd" (III. 269–70) for Man's restoration:

> Admiration seiz'd
> All Heav'n, what this might mean, and whither tend
> Wond'ring.
>
> (III. 271–73)

It is at the conclusion of the Father's speech, which provides
an answer to the angels' silent query, "what this might mean,"
that the angelic silence is finally broken by

>   all
> The multitude of Angels with a shout
> Loud as from numbers without number, sweet
> As from blest voices, uttering joy, Heav'n rung
> With Jubilee, and loud Hosannas fill'd
> Th' eternal Regions.
>
> (III. 344–49)

The contrast with the preceding moment of silence is superbly
rendered by the poet in these sonorous lines with their effect
of total rapturous acclamation.

The genuineness of the joyous angelic outburst is underscored by the Father's promised exaltation of the Son (III.
305–19), and the Father's promise is, in turn, based upon the
Son's exemplary demonstration of

>   immortal love
> To mortal men, above which only shone
> Filial obedience.
>
> (III. 267–69)

As the Father emphasizes during His final speech to the Son,
it is the Son's exemplary response to His inducing challenge

that demonstrates the Son's "immortal love" and His "filial obedience," and which justly *merits* His exaltation:

> Because thou hast, though Thron'd in highest bliss
> Equal to God, and equally enjoying
> God-like fruition, quitted all to save
> A world from utter loss, *and hast been found*
> *By Merit more than Birthright Son of God,*
> *Found worthiest to be so by being Good,*
> *Far more than Great or High;* because in thee
> Love hath abounded more than Glory abounds,
> Therefore thy Humiliation shall exalt
> With thee thy Manhood also to this Throne;
> Here shalt thou sit incarnate, here shalt Reign
> Both God and Man, Son both of God and Man,
> Anointed universal King; all Power
> I give thee, reign for ever, and *assume*
> *Thy Merits.*
>
> (III. 305–19)[57]

The *logical* juxtaposition of "hast been found / By Merit" and "assume / Thy Merits" best establishes, in terms of both language and structure, the basic rationale of the entire scene. For by placing the emphasis (at the climax of the Father's speeches in Book III) on the Son's meritorious conduct, the poet is able, within the context of the developing drama, to integrate several crucial elements of the scene into a coherent poetic unity. For example, by placing the emphasis on *merit* in His final speech to the Son, the Father, in fact, employs categories and values that belong essentially to the visible world where the discursive mode—which, as a matter of fact, He has used throughout His appearance in the scene (in His verbal exchanges with the Son)—is paramount.

Clearly, the Father, characterized by the angelic choir as

---

57. Italics mine.

> Omnipotent,
> Immutable, Immortal, Infinite,
> Eternal King . . . Author of all being,
> Fountain of Light, thyself invisible
> . . . .
> Thron'd inaccessible,
>
>   (III. 372–77)

need not utter a syllable to His Son, in whom "all his Father
shone / Substantially express'd" (III. 139–40), in order to
communicate His Will to His invariably attentive Son (see, for
example, III. 269–71). But He does; and He does so in a
manner that not only utilizes the discursive mode, but also
sanctions the categories and values of the visible world (wit-
ness, for instance, the Father's Great Question to *all* the
"Heav'nly Powers" in III. 213–16, as well as His emphasis on
merit in His final speech). Notwithstanding Milton's obvious
poetic need to portray the God of *Paradise Lost* in *reasonably*
comprehensible terms, such a need would appear to be less
important than the portrait of a God who, paradoxically, must
be challengingly severe in order to effect a demonstration by
the Son (of the latter's "immortal love" and "Filial obedience")
that is both *comprehensible* and *exemplary*—to "Heav'nly Powers" and to human readers alike.

   This is exactly the effect that the poet achieves by making
the burden of the scene the climactic emphasis on merit toward the end of the Father's final speech. By focusing on the
Son's *demonstration* of His "immortal love" and "Filial obedience" (attested to by the Father's exaltation of the Son on the
basis of the latter's *earned* reward), the poet is able to unify the
various elements of language, drama, imagery, and character
throughout the scene, disclosing (through the climactic emphasis on merit) the enacted process that leads logically to the
Father's exaltation, and to the angels' acclamation, of the Son.
For, by placing the emphasis on merit during His concluding

speech to the Son, the Father is, in fact, suggesting both an acceptable performance by the Son, which effects that merit, and a frame of reference against which that performance may be assessed. Ultimately, that performance is the exemplary conduct of the Son, the result of the enacted drama of induced choice; and the frame of reference is the Father Himself, who not only is, as the Son declares, "Judge / Of all things made, and judgest only right" (III. 154–55), but who also sets the stage for the enacted drama (even before the Son's direct participation in the scene) with His incipient restorative intention:

> Man falls deceiv'd
> By th' other first: Man therefore shall find grace,
> The other none: in Mercy and Justice both,
> Through Heav'n and Earth, so shall my glory excel,
> *But Mercy first and last shall brightest shine.*
> (III. 130–34)[58]

"Mercy first and last shall brightest shine" because everything begins with the Father and ends in Him. For He is the creative and restorative reason for every merciful and right choice. Yet, because He is "Immutable, Immortal, Infinite," the Father is also "thron'd inaccessible." Consequently, it is through the agency of the Son, the Father's Word, Wisdom, and Effectual Might (see III. 170), that the Father actualizes His inaccessible and essentially incomprehensible creative and restorative purposes toward Man. But in order to do so, He chooses (as the poet demonstrates in Book III) to implement His purposes in discursively accessible and logically comprehensible ways.

But more than that, as the "Author of all being," the "Judge / Of all things made," the Father also exercises com-

---

58. Italics mine.

plete control over, and readily sanctions, even these less than intuitively rational means. For one thing, as Raphael explains to Adam (V. 486–90), the difference between the discursive and the intuitive modes is merely one of degree, not of kind. Significantly, it is the Father Himself who instructs Raphael, immediately before the latter's departure on his mission to the prelapsarian Adam, to

> Converse with Adam . . .
> . . . and such discourse bring on,
> As may advise him of his happy state.
> (V. 230–34)[59]

Despite the obvious differences between Adam and the Son, the Father's mode of communication with the Son in Book III clearly demonstrates His own intention to "converse. . . . and such discourse bring on" as may best illustrate the practical pattern of exemplary "filial obedience" and "charity . . . dear." For, however much the poet may have wished to "see and tell / Of things invisible to mortal sight" (III. 54–55), it would surely never have escaped him that "our understanding cannot in this body found itself but on sensible things," and that

> the Acts of God . . .
> . . . to human ears
> Cannot without procéss of speech be told,
> So told as earthly notion can receive.
> (VII. 176–79)

In the end, it is from this sensible perspective of the human condition, enacted in *Paradise Lost* through an inescapably discursive accessibility, that the poet succeeds in portraying a world "of things invisible to mortal sight," a world in which

---

59. Italics mine.

the central, paradoxical capability of the Son functions continuously to unify and fuse the poem's circular structure and its illogical insistence on the creative and restorative nature of God's ways.

Bibliography

Adamson, J. H. "The War in Heaven: *The Merkabah.*" In *Bright Essence: Studies in Milton's Theology*, edited by W. B. Hunter, C. A. Patrides, and J. H. Adamson. Salt Lake City, Utah: University of Utah Press, 1971.

Allison, C. F. *The Rise of Moralism*. New York: The Seabury Press, 1966.

Aquinas, Thomas. *The Summa Theologica*. Translated by Fathers of the English Dominican Province, and revised by Daniel J. Sullivan. 2 vols. *Great Books of the Western World*, edited by Robert Maynard Hutchins, vols. 19 and 20. Chicago, Ill.: Encyclopaedia Britannica Inc., 1952.

Augustine. *The City of God*. Translated by Marcus Dods. *Great Books of the Western World*, by Robert Maynard Hutchins, vol. 18. Chicago, Ill.: Encyclopaedia Britannica, Inc., 1952.

Barker, Arthur E. *Milton and the Puritan Dilemma: 1641–1660*. Toronto: University of Toronto Press, 1942.

————. "*Paradise Lost:* The Relevance of Regeneration." In *Paradise Lost: A Tercentenary Tribute*, edited by Balachandra Rajan. Toronto: Univeristy of Toronto Press, 1969.

————. "Structural and Doctrinal Pattern in Milton's Later Poems." In *Essays in English Literature from the Renaissance to the Victorian Age*, edited by Millar MacLure and F. W. Watt. Toronto: University of Toronto Press, 1964.

Baxter, Richard. *The Saints' Everlasting Rest.* London, 1650.

———. *Sermons,* edited by Thomas W. Jenkyn. London: Thomas Nelson, 1846.

———. *The Practical Works of Richard Baxter.* vol. 3. London: G. Virtue, 1838.

Bromiley, Geoffrey W., ed. and trans. *Theological Dictionary of the New Testament.* Former editor: Gerdard Kittel. vol. 2. Grand Rapids, Mich.: Wm. B. Eerdmans Publishing Company, 1964.

Burden, Dennis H. *The Logical Epic: A Study of the Argument of Paradise Lost.* Cambridge, Mass.: Harvard University Press, 1967.

Bush, Douglas. *"Paradise Lost" in Our Time.* Ithaca, N.Y.: Cornell University Press, 1945.

Calvin, John. *Institutes of the Christian Religion.* vol. 2. Translated by John Allen. Philadelphia: The Westminster Press, 1936.

———. *Institutes of the Christian Religion.* Translated by H. Beveridge. Edinburg, 1875.

———. *Theological Treatises.* Translated by J. K. S. Reid, The Library of Christian Classics. vol. 22. Philadelphia: The Westminster Press, 1954.

Clark, Ira. "Milton and the Image of God." *JEGP* 68 (July 1969): 422–31.

Coffin, Charles M. "Creation and the Self in *Paradise Lost.*" *ELH* 29 (1962): 1–18.

Colie, Rosalie L. *Paradoxia Epidemica: The Renaissance Tradition of Paradox.* Princeton, N. J.: Princeton University Press, 1966.

Collins, Dan Stead. *Rhetoric and Logic in Milton's English Poems.* Ann Arbor, Mich.: University Microfilms, Inc., 1969.

Coolidge, John S. *The Pauline Renaissance in England.* London: Oxford University Press, 1970.

Cormican, L. A. "Milton's Religious Verse." *The Pelican Guide to English Literature: From Donne to Marvell.* Edited by Boris Ford. vol. 3. Baltimore, Md.: Penguin Books, 1956.

Cudworth, Ralph. *A Sermon Preached before the Honourable House of Commons.* March 31, 1647.

Diekhoff, John S. *Milton on Himself.* London: Cohen & West, Ltd., 1965.

Dodd, C. Harold. *The Meaning of Paul for Today.* London: Fontana Books, 1958.

Eaton, John. *The Honey-Combe of Free Justification.* London, 1642.

Empson, William. *Milton's God.* London: Chatto & Windus, 1961.

Encyclopedia Judaica. vol. 10. New York: The Macmillan Co., 1971.

Evans, J. M. *Paradise Lost and the Genesis Tradition.* London: Oxford University Press, 1968.

Fish, Stanley E. "Discovery as Form in *Paradise Lost.*" *New Essays on Paradise Lost,* by Thomas Kranidas. Berkeley and Los Angeles: University of California Press, 1969.

————. "Inaction and Silence: The Reader in *Paradise Regained.*" *Calm of Mind: Tercentenary Essays on Paradise Regained and Samson Agonistes in honor of John S. Diekhoff,* by Joseph Anthony Wittreich, Jr. Cleveland, Ohio: Case Western Reserve University Press, 1971.

————. *Surprised by Sin: the Reader in Paradise Lost.* New York: St. Martin's Press, 1967.

Fisher, Edward. *The Marrow of Modern Divinity.* 19th edition, with notes by Thomas Boston Montrose. London: D. Buchanan, 1803.

Fixler, Michael. *Milton and the Kingdoms of God.* London: Faber & Faber, 1964.

Fletcher, Harris Francis. *Milton's Rabbinical Readings.* Urbana, Ill.: University of Illinois Press, 1930.

Frye, Northrup. *The Return of Eden.* Toronto: University of Toronto Press, 1965.

Frye, Roland Mushat. *God, Man, and Satan.* Princeton, N.J.: Princeton University Press, 1960.

Gardner, Dame Helen. *A Reading of Paradise Lost.* London: Oxford University Press, 1965.

Gataker, Thomas. *Antinomianism Discovered and Confuted.* London, 1652.

Gilbert, Allan H. *On the Composition of Paradise Lost.* New York: Octagon Books, Inc., 1966.

Goodwin, John. *Certain briefe Observations and Antiquaeries: on Master Prin's Twelve Questions about Church-government.* London, 1644.

_____. *Imputatio Fidei*. London, 1642.

_____. *Innocency and Truth Triumphing together*. London, 1645.

_____. *The Divine Authority of the Scriptures Asserted*. London, 1648.

Grace, William J. *Ideas in Milton*. Notre Dame, Ind.: University of Notre Dame Press, 1968.

Grose, Christopher. *Milton's Epic Process: Paradise Lost and Its Miltonic Background*. New Haven, Conn.: Yale University Press, 1973.

Haller, William. *Liberty and Reformation in the Puritan Revolution*. New York: Columbia University Press, 1955.

_____. *The Rise of Puritanism*. New York: Harper and Brothers, 1938.

Hamilton, G. Rostrevor. *Hero or Fool?* Folcroft, Pa.: The Folcroft Press, Inc., 1944; reprinted 1969.

Hanford, James Holly. *John Milton: Poet and Humanist*. Cleveland, Ohio: The Press of Western Reserve University, 1966.

Hastings, James, ed. *Encyclopedia of Religion and Ethics*. vols. 4 and 10. New York: Charles Scribner's Sons, 1961.

Hughes, Merritt Y., ed. *John Milton: Complete Poems and Major Prose*. New York: The Odyssey Press, 1957.

_____. *Ten Perspectives on Milton*. New Haven, Conn.: Yale University Press, 1965.

Hyman, Lawrence W. *The Quarrel Within*. Port Washington, N.Y.: Kennikat Press, Inc., 1972.

Ingram, William and Swaim, Kathleen, eds. *A Concordance to Milton's English Poetry*. London: Oxford University Press, 1972.

Kelley, Maurice. *This Great Argument: A Study of Milton's De Doctrina Christiana as a Gloss upon Paradise Lost*. Princeton, N. J.: Princeton University Press, 1941.

Knappen, M. M. *Tudor Puritanism: A Chapter in the History of Idealism*. Chicago, Ill.: The University of Chicago Press, 1939; reprinted 1965.

Kranidas, Thomas. *The Fierce Equation: A Study of Milton's Decorum*. The Hague, 1965.

Lawry, Jon S. *The Shadow of Heaven: Matter and Stance in Milton's Poetry*. Ithaca, N.Y.: Cornell University Press, 1968.

Lewis, C. S. *A Preface to Paradise Lost*. London: Oxford University Press, 1942.

————. *The Problem of Pain*. London: Fontana Books, 1957. First published, London: Geoffrey Bles, 1940.

MacCaffrey, Isabel G. "The Theme of *Paradise Lost*, Book III." In *New Essays on Paradise Lost*, by Thomas Kranidas. Berkeley and Los Angeles, Calif.: University of California Press, 1969.

Madsen, William G. "Earth the Shadow of Heaven: Typological Symbolism in *Paradise Lost*." *PMLA* 75 (1960): 519–26; reprinted in *Milton: Modern Essays in Criticism*, by Arthur E. Barker. New York: Oxford University Press, 1965, pp. 246–63.

Murray, Patrick. *Milton: The Modern Phase*. New York: Barnes & Noble, Inc., 1967.

Neal, Daniel. *The History of the Puritans*. Revised, Corrected, and Enlarged, with additional Notes by John O. Choules. 2 vols. New York: Harper & Brothers, 1843.

New Catholic Encyclopedia. vol. 4. Edited by The Catholic University of America. New York: McGraw-Hill, Inc., 1967.

Parker, William Riley. *Milton's Contemporary Reputation*. New York: Haskell House Publishers, Ltd., 1971.

Patrides, C. A. "The Godhead in *Paradise Lost:* Dogma or Drama? In *Bright Essence: Studies in Milton's Theology*, edited by W. B. Hunter, C. A. Patrides, and J. H. Adamson. Salt Lake City: University of Utah Press, 1971.

————. *Milton and the Christian Tradition*. London: Oxford University Press, 1966.

————, ed. *Milton's Epic Poetry: Essays on Paradise Lost and Paradise Regained*. London: Penguin Books, 1967.

————. "*Paradise Lost* and the Language of Theology." In *Language and Style in Milton: A Symposium in Honor of the Tercentenary of Paradise Lost*, edited by David Emma and John T. Shawcross. New York: Frederick Ungar Publishing Company, Inc., 1967.

Patterson, Frank Allen, ed. *The Student's Milton*. New York: Appleton-Century-Crofts, Inc., 1961.

Peter, John. *A Critique of Paradise Lost*. Hamden, Conn.: Archon Books, 1970.

Plato. *The Dialogues and the Seventh Letter*. Translated by Benjamin Jowett and J. Harward. *Great Books of the Western World*, edited by Robert Maynard Hutchins. Chicago, Ill.: Encyclopaedia Britannica, Inc., 1952.

Prince, F. T. "On the Last Two Books of *Paradise Lost.*" In *Milton's Epic Poetry: Essays on Paradise Lost and Paradise Regained*, by C. A. Patrides, London: Penguin Books, 1967.

Rajan, Balachandra, ed. *Milton's Paradise Lost: Books I and II.* New York: Asia Publishing House, 1964.

―――. *Paradise Lost and the Seventeenth Century Reader.* London: Chatto & Windus, 1947.

―――. *"Paradise Lost:* The Web of Responsibility." In *Paradise Lost: A Tercentenary Tribute*, by Balachandra Rajan. Toronto: University of Toronto Press, 1969.

―――. "Simple, Sensuous and Passionate." *RES* 21 (1945): 289–301; reprinted in *Milton: Modern Essays in Criticism*, by Arthur E. Barker. New York: Oxford Univeristy Press, 1965, pp. 3–20.

Reuter, Karl. *William Ames; the leading theologian in the awakening of reformed pietism.* Translated by Douglas Horton. Cambridge, 1965. German edition: Neukirchen, Neukirchener Verlag, 1940.

Revard, Stella P. "The Dramatic Function of the Son in *Paradise Lost:* A Commentary on Milton's 'Trinitarianism.' " *JEGP* 66 (1967): 45–58.

Richardson, Jonathan. *The Life of Milton, and a Discourse on Paradise Lost* (1734). In *The Early Lives of Milton*, edited Helen Darbishire. London: Constable & Co., Ltd., 1932.

Riggs, William G. "The Poet and Satan in *Paradise Lost.*" In *Milton Studies II*, by James D. Simmonds. Pittsburgh, Pa.: University of Pittsburgh Press, 1970.

Rolston, Holmes. *John Calvin versus The Westminster Confession.* Richmond, Va.: John Knox Press, 1972.

Samuel, Irene. *Dante and Milton: The Commedia and Paradise Lost.* Ithaca, N.Y.: Cornell University Press, 1966.

―――. "The Dialogue in Heaven: A Reconsideration of *Paradise Lost*, *III. 1–417.*" In *Milton: Modern Essays in Criticism*, by Arthur E. Barker. London: Oxford University Press, 1965.

―――. *"Paradise Lost* as Mimesis." *Approaches to Paradise Lost: The York Tercentenary Lectures*, by C. A. Patrides. Toronto: University of Toronto Press, 1968.

Schenk, W. *The Concern for Social Justice in the Puritan Revolution.* London: Longmans, Green and Company, 1948.

Scott, William A. *Historical Protestantism: An Historical Introduction to Protestant Theology.* Englewood Cliffs, N.J.: Prentice-Hall, Inc., 1971.

Seaman, John E. *The Moral Paradox of Paradise Lost.* The Hague: Mouton & Co, N.V., Publishers, 1971.

Sims, James H. *The Bible in Milton's Epics.* Gainesville, Fla.: University of Florida Press, 1962.

Sprunger, Keith L. *The Learned Doctor William Ames.* Urbana, Ill.: University of Illinois Press, 1972.

Steadman, J. M. "Heroic Virtue and the Divine Image in *Paradise Lost.*" *JWCI* 22 (1959): 88–105.

Stein, Arnold. *Answerable Style: Essays on Paradise Lost.* Minneapolis, Minn.: University of Minnesota Press, 1953.

Summers, Joseph H. *The Muse's Method: An Introduction to Paradise Lost.* Cambridge, Mass.: Harvard University Press, 1962.

Tillyard, E. M. W. *Milton.* rev. ed. London: Chatto & Windus, 1966.

————. *The Miltonic Setting: Past and Present.* London: Barnes & Noble, Inc., 1966. First published London: Chatto & Windus, Ltd., 1938.

————. *Studies in Milton.* London: Chatto & Windus, 1960.

Waldock, A. J. A. *Paradise Lost and Its Critics.* Cambridge: Cambridge University Press, 1947.

Walker, D. P. *The Ancient Theology.* Ithaca, N.Y.: Cornell University Press, 1972.

————. *The Decline of Hell.* Chicago: The University of Chicago Press, 1964.

Werblowsky, R. J. Zwi. *Lucifer and Prometheus: A Study of Milton's Satan.* London: Routledge & Kegan Paul, Ltd., 1952.

West, Robert H. *Milton and the Angels.* Athens, Ga.: University of Georgia Press, 1955.

Whichcote, Benjamin. *Moral and Religious Aphorisms.* London, 1930.

Wilding, Michael. *Milton's Paradise Lost.* Sydney: Sydney University Press, 1969.

Willey, Basil. *The Seventeenth Century Background*. New York: Doubleday & Co., Inc., 1953. First published, 1934.

Williams, Charles. *Reason and Beauty in the Poetic Mind*. London: Oxford University Press, 1933.

Willis, E. David. *Calvin's Catholic Christology*. Leiden.: E. J. Brill Publishing Company, 1966.

Woodhouse, A. S. P., ed. *Puritanism and Liberty*. London: J. M. Dent & Sons, Ltd., 1965. First published, 1938.

Zweig, Stefan. *The Right to Heresy: Castellio against Calvin*. Translated by Eden and Cedar Paul. New York: The Viking Press, 1936.

Index

Adam: and God's justice, 141–45; curse of, 144; God's creative testing of, 141–43; in Calvin's theology, 49, 54, 99; in Milton's theology, 79, 83; laughed at by Satan, 116; loyalty of, 120; Michael's conversation with, in *PL*, 118, 155, 161–67, 187–93; post-lapsarian condition of, 145, 197; prohibition against, 117; Raphael's conversation with, in *PL*, 118, 151, 180, 182–84, 192, 195–96, 208; responsibility of, 144; Son's judgment of, 143–45, 189–90
Adamson, J. H., 139
Allison, C. F., 114
Ames, William, 44, 58–62
An Apology for Smectymnuus, 169, 175
Antinomianism: characteristics of, 64, 68, 71, 95; excesses of, 45, 63, 70, 100
Aquinas, Saint, 151
Areopagitica, 19, 22, 79–80, 121, 158
Arminianism, 45, 67
Augustine, Saint, 17, 28, 44, 53, 85, 98, 151

Barker, Arthur E., 27, 33–35, 75, 147
Baxter, Richard, 44, 45, 59, 63–68

Beza, Theodore, 103
Bible: accuracy of, 45, 51, 84, 88, 94–96; Genevan, 103; New Testament, references to, 45, 68, 86, 91–98, 99–100, 102–7, 139; Old Testament, references to, 45, 52, 86–92, 96–97, 102, 104, 139; study of, 66, 83, 94; view of, 74
Biblical God: grace of, 101, 122; judgment of, 101; love of, 103; righteousness of, 86, 91–98, 101–2, 104, 106–7; Son of, 95–96, 106–7; will of, 100, 103; word of, 100–101. *See also* Calvinists' God; Milton's God
Broadbent, J. B., 24
Bromiley, Geoffrey W., 95
Brown, W. Adams, 98–99
Bunyan, John, 45
Burden, Dennis, 178
Bush, Douglas, 174, 196

Calvin, John, 46–55
Calvinism: influence of, 46–47; orthodox, 45–47, 55–62, 78, 83
Calvinists' God: judgment of, 50–52, 64–65; revelation of, 48–49, 62, 67; will of, 49–50, 52–53, 60–62, 68,

219